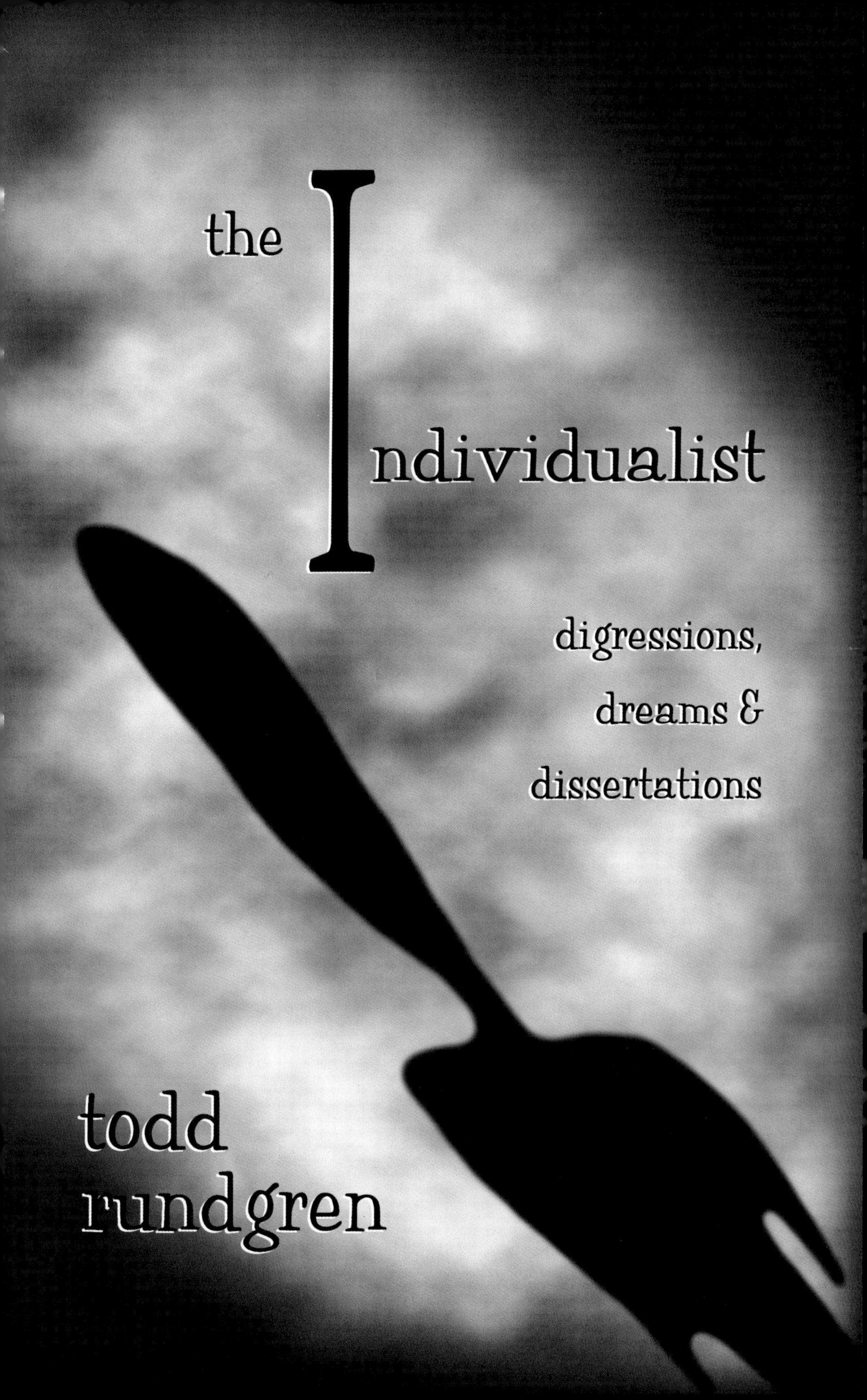

the Individualist

digressions,
dreams &
dissertations

todd
rundgren

CLEOPATRA

Cleopatra Press
11041 Santa Monica Blvd. #703 Los Angeles, CA 90025
ISBN:
978-0-9972056-5-7
Printed in Hong Kong

Cover art and layout design by Todd Rundgren
Back cover photo by Lynn Goldsmith
Production layout by Fendi Nugroho

The Individualist
Digressions, Dreams & Dissertations

Todd Rundgren

CONTENTS

a note about form:

I was asked to write a book about myself and took it under consideration when I realized that if I didn't do it, someone else might and I would certainly not agree with the result. After I thought about it further I realized that the exercise might pass for entertainment and since that violated no precedent, I put myself to the task of actually remembering and transcribing what had happened to me. It did not take long to conclude that I would not be able to organize the mess without some formal self-discipline. Know thyself.

Rooting around in my subconscious for meaningful reminiscences is not necessarily my definition of a day well spent since I'm so preoccupied with what I'm experiencing now. But then perhaps that's the point of paying attention now- so one can remember well later in one's immobile years. Yet the more I think about the process the more a certain paralysis sets in, likely triggered by the fact that it reminds me of a high school homework assignment and jeez do I never want to go through that again.

So in order to get myself and the reader through this process with a minimum of chaos, the book will take on the form of this page: a recollection of something that I witnessed, a subjective assessment of my state of mind in either experiencing or remembering the episode (or a haphazard combination of both), and as in this paragraph a conclusion, a statement of plain facts or simply soapbox proselytizing. I suggest scanning the book in whatever manner one's taste and temperament dictate. The story is only part finished, anyway.

Baba

When Baba started wandering out of her room and falling down the staircase late at night because she forgot it was there, it became pretty obvious that she had to go to a nursing home. It wasn't too far from my parents house in Bywood- even closer to the Westbrook Park row house I grew up in, and seemed a reasonable enough place as such depressing institutions go. Rex was about four when we went over for a visit and she started calling him Jerry, a name nobody in the family recognized. Then for about an hour she talked about stuff that had happened to her over the past 80 or so years and showed me pictures of her and a lot of other mostly women in a sweater factory in the thirties, remembering the names of most of the people and something about their character or behavior. I learned things about the long lost namesake of the family, her husband, who split when my dad was still a kid because he claimed he was dying of lung disease, and all the rumors about possible significant Swedish connections around the turn of the century somewhere in the bloodline. The only thing I remember about my Mom's dad is that when I was Rex's age he used to pull out his false teeth and scare the shit out of me. He was gone shortly thereafter.

There are memories of my own that I find suspicious in that they may be something that happened in consensus reality or something that I dreamed or imagined. It's really only a problem if it causes you to believe in something at variance with the consensus. Otherwise, the remembrances are seamlessly mingled and equally fuzzy. On the basis of such evidence, what can I believe about a man who's entire spiritual legacy to me is the memory of false teeth, naked gums and floppy lips?

Something about aging, perhaps the growing insensitivity of the body, causes the past to become progressively clearer as the present defocuses. Would that one could control that field of view and recall in vivid detail the truly epiphanal moments in one's life in all their sensuality and naïveté. That's when you start falling down the staircase.

Birth

According to my mother Ruth (the only one who would have re-membered), my labor lasted three days because my head was so big it got wedged in her pelvis, a situation that became apparently life threatening for one or the both of us. She pointed out a dent in the crown of my skull as proof of the ordeal, but I have no other memory of it. Nor of the days in a Philadelphia apartment where I projectile puked my way through early infancy. She recalled nights locked in the tiny bathroom while my dad played cards with friends and I firehosed the water closet with formula. The earliest memory that she and I dared to share was of her screaming and banging my head against a wall after I, newly ambulatory, had learned to fill the hamper with water transported from the bathroom sink. We've had a chuckle or two over that one, assuming there was no permanent damage. At least no one's ever proved there was.

My mother recalls a vivid dream she had while in the delirium of my protracted labor: She and I and my dad are floating on a cloud. I haven't been born yet but she knows it's me. I am telling her that everything is going to be peaceful and wonderful and she begins to feel that everything is. I tell her that great planet-shaping things are going to happen to us, and she believes they will. It sounds wonder-ful, like a dream I'd enjoy having.

Some who have met my mother in later years are probably skep-tical that she would ever be capable of an act of violence such as banging my head against the wall. I've never held a grudge about it, although that kind of thing can stand out in your mind. It was one of a number episodes where she freaked herself out more than me and never repeated the behavior. Nobody, particularly not my forebears, ever talked about the reality of having and raising kids. My mom's mother was a cool, judgmental, biblically pious wom-an- my dad's father disappeared before he was in his teens. I feel bad about the quietly torturous ignorance they had to suffer from childhood well past parenthood. Me, I would have to conclude that there is something significant, in a traveling carnival sideshow kind of way, about my head and the events that have 'impacted' it.

Westbrook

After about a year of being a struggling family man, my dad found us a place in a postwar housing development west of the city- 323 Westbrook Drive, a brick rowhouse of the kind that is common in the northeast: three bedrooms, one bath, kitchen, dining, living room, basement, garage. We had a front yard, a parking space in back and a share of the island that occupied the filling of the candy bar that was the neighborhood's geography, replicated like bacteria over acres and acres. The 'rows' were like apartment buildings that had fallen down. Your neighbors were not directly over and under you, but directly next to you. Vendors plied the back driveways- the produce huckster and the guy who sharpened scissors- and the front drives- the ice cream man and the kids offering to paint your house number on the curb. Summer brought carousels mounted on truck beds and the chance run in the toxic billows of Japanese beetle extermination sprayers that would just appear unannounced, because they were eating everyones roses I guess. In the winter I hogged the heat vent nearest the TV and avoided the outdoors.

Growing up in Westbrook Park, I was incognizant of the fact that we were living where few white folk had lived before. At least if anything had been there it was wiped out and paved over. The trees and lawns and flower bushes were no older than I was. The screen doors that provided the only character from house to house were mostly younger than I. We were settlers on the frontier that was suburbia. We were the future, but how was I to know? I only lived for the sound of the ice cream truck rolling down the narrow street.

It's hard to imagine a time before suburbia. Not long ago urban boundaries ended and then you were in the countryside. People lived where they worked, which was either a factory or a farm. The 'convenience' of the automobile just blurred the crap out of everything- how far from your job you could live, but also property rights as highways were built, economics as a planet became addicted to carbon, and of course, the fetid atmosphere.

Music

My parents had an RCA 45 RPM player that probably was supposed to be shared but which I hogged at an early age. You could stack about 8 singles on the fat spindle, Capitol recordings of the Boston Pops Orchestra playing light classics like Chicken Reel and Skaters Waltz. Many of the discs were colored vinyl which I would stare through as the music played for hours. I'd sometimes sit in the kitchenette and listen to the radio while my mother cooked and sang along with Patti Page and Johnny Mathis. So-called Rock & Roll had not yet been recognized a genre and my parents had somewhat conservative tastes so there was never anything like jazz being played. There was music on the TV, like Perry Como and Mitch Miller and occasionally something interesting on Ed Sullivan. Then my dad built his own HiFi from plans in Popular Electronics so we began to hear LPs of classical music and show tunes, long form music which kept me rapt for as long as my dad would listen-he would never let me touch the turntable. I eventually got a crappy portable stereo of my own so that I could start buying the records I wanted to hear.

I was a bit indignant that I couldn't use my dad's HiFi, but I had no complaints with his musical preferences. Not a lot of the 3 Bs and thankfully, no Wagner. Ravel and DeBussy, Rimsky-Korsakov and Stravinsky, passionate and accessible composers as well as lots of show music. Oddly, not many soloists- more likely comedy by somebody like Bob Newhart or the Smothers Brothers. And The New Christy Minstrels because we all liked Hootenanny on the TV looky box.

I credit my dad with whatever musical sophistication I possess. The somewhat strict ban on certain music exposed me to a broader range of ways to express. There is an entirely other effect created by wordless music, when the composer must paint a picture in the listeners mind using sound alone. The giants of the late 19th and early 20th centuries created the language we still depend on today, the refrains that transform mute plays into emotionally underscored films, cuing everyone how they are supposed to feel at every moment. Sometimes the lyric just takes the air out of everything.

Kindergarten

Westbrook Park was such a spankin' new development that they had yet to finish building the elementary school so I had to be bussed to kindergarten in another township. I hated the very idea of going to school, every part of the socialization process frightened me from the time I got on the bus through the hours of classroom and awkward lunches and feeling relief only as I step off the bus again. I was easily bored and would wind up often being shuttled to the back of the class. My only respite was recess because the school adjoined a wooded area with a stream running through it. This was my daily destination and afforded me a closer look at nature than the artificiality of Westbrook Park. I was prone to tantrums and one day I got it into my head that I was going to walk home, which was several miles away and I thought I could find from following the bus route, and was halfway out the front door when the principal ran out and grabbed me. Everyone is starting to realize now that something is not altogether right with me and things are not going to get easier. School and I were going to have a very rocky relationship.

I've never known how smart I am, which I guess was a problem for me, but more so for those who had to raise me. I wasn't stupid, but this was a time before 'learning disorders' and everyone around you thinks you can control yourself. I was pretty quick at learning things but that didn't translate into an interest in sitting in a classroom listening to someone drone at me. None of it seemed to have context- why are they trying to make me learn this? Let me do something frivolous and figure out what I need to learn in order to do it. I wanna build a robot!

Socialization and standardization are legitimate goals. People need to learn some basis for getting along with others and being able to have cogent communication with them. Education is much more problematic because in fact people do not learn at exactly the same pace and in exactly the same way. That's when school becomes a factory for creating consumers, to which our parents gladly bus us off so they do not go insane from our constant presence. As a kid I thought home schooling would be great because no bus, no boredom, no bullies. In retrospect, that would have been a formula for disaster... or worse!

Randolph

It was a brand new Westbrook Park Elementary School, close enough to our house that we could walk there. Two stories of tan brick and glass block, modern and faceless. The classrooms started with kindergarten at one end of the lower floor, advancing to third grade at the other, then starting with fourth grade on the second floor over kindergarten… you get the idea. I finished out a few months of K there then returned triumphantly a first-grader sitting at a real desk of my own, a podium from which expectations are suddenly much higher. One day I am, as usual, the last to enter my classroom and glance down the hall to the next doorway and there's a kid standing there and we're the only two kids in the hall and we start laughing. Randy Read. Simpatico. Our 'relationship' blossomed especially as I found his home to be a haven from the strife of my life. Randy's mother doted on him at the expense of the rest of his family and as years passed more of the household resources would be turned over to him. Their basement and garage was eventually converted into a bachelor pad for him and his brother Collie, but as I grew older Collie was eventually banished to another part of the house since I started regularly sleeping over. This room became the lab for all manner of mischief- for once I was not the instigator of trouble, merely a collaborator with a partner who somehow had access to the resources that enabled our nefarious deeds. And Randy got good grades, unlike myself, so we had a collective cover I never could have created for myself. If it was a dare he came up with, I was in- nobody was going to ground Randy.

I hadn't thought about it at the time, but Randy was the first friend I ever made in school. The kind that you have for life. There were other kids I might have hung with but kind of fell out of friendship as time wore on. I do remember Harry Bruner who was also kind of a loner. I spent time with him because his dad was a jeweler and we would steal sulfuric acid from his office and do weird things with it to see what it would dissolve, but I must have lost interest when we ran out of chemicals.

Maybe most people go through life without having a 'special friend', someone who shares all the mysteries of growing up and sees the world as you do: a place not to be taken seriously. Somebody not just to spend time with and have a laugh, but to scheme great schemes with, to encourage to greater acts of foolishness, to challenge the world. The kind of friend your parents would tell you to stay away from but for the fact that it is pretty much your only friend.

June

Three weeks before my first birthday June was born. One of my first memories is of her and me in the hospital to have our tonsils removed, which I guess was either trendy or a bargain. We were sharing the room with another kid in the 3 to 4 age group whom we never really got to know because of the production line quality of the experience. One by one we were plucked from the tiny ward and transported to the mysterious beyond. June was first to go. After about 15 minutes I couldn't stand the suspense any longer and snuck out into the hall. The operating room was a door or two away and I cracked it just in time to see the masked zombies pointing what seemed to be a vacuum cleaner nozzle with sparks coming out the end down unconscious June's little throat. I fled back to the ward and waited in terror until the prep nurse came in, at which point I begged her to take the other kid. No dice. I'm placed on a gurney and rolled into the hall where a guy tells me I'm going to play Santa Claus, and he covers my face with a ball of white gauze. When I awaken it's dark and I have a terrible sore throat. I find my way into the hall and over to a water fountain where I guzzle stuporously. A nurse sees me and tells me I should be in my room, just seconds before I puke blood all over the hallway.

One of the creepiest experiences of my life was my first whiff of ether. It's cold and has an electric/chemical smell and knocks you out like you've been smacked in the head with a wrecking ball. After it wore off, I had a different feeling about myself, like I had been shown some great weakness that would stalk me forever in the form of that chemical odor. I imagine it's very much like nerve gas would smell. And the memory of those hospital creatures boring down June's 4 year old throat after her tiny tonsils is creepier than any episode of X Files I've seen thus far.

You might assume that shared traumas would bring siblings closer together, but in retrospect it would require much more than twofer tonsillectomies to quell rivalry in a family where affection was such a rare commodity. June and I were never very close. To this day I'm sure she and I don't understand each other. I'm not even sure we like each other. Shared joy is a common bond. Shared unpleasantness is still suffered alone. Guess you can't help but take it personally.

Teeth

One day when I was 5 or 6 I was pedaling my tricycle around the empty lot near the house and leaning over the handlebars hypnotized by the front wheel when I hit a rock or something and landed teeth first into that hypnotic wheel. Came home crying and bloody where mom and Nana made a cursory diagnosis that I was still a baby. A week or two later my front teeth turned brown and that was the beginning of a lifetime of dental issues. Apparently the brownness is due to the fact that the teeth have actually died which means the blood vessels that would normally dissolve the roots of your baby teeth are gone so when your big boy teeth start to grow in, instead of pushing out your stubby baby toofs, the roots thereof get pushed through your gums and I could go into further disgusting detail but the end result is not optimal dental-wise. Complicate that with a visit to some mystery tonsure who decided to extract a permanent molar, even as my teeth are growing in so now everything on the bottom is moving sideways to fill in the gap. Baba put up the money to send me to an orthodontist and for about 2 of my late elementary years I wore every manner of bizarre construction and device of torture to presumably undo the original accident, all to no avail. My bite became so uneven that tiny fissures appeared in my molars causing them to crumble over time. We had no dental plan for such catastrophes.

I don't remember if I was self conscious about my teeth before- my hair was more of a fixation. From that moment on I realized my teeth were going to look stupid and I would look stupid if I didn't adapt to that fact. Keep your mouth closed when taking pictures. You can smile, just keep your lips closed. Don't laugh like a jackass if you can help it- best not to laugh like a jackass anyway. Try to have fun with it, like doing tongue tricks with the gap between your front teeth.

Teeth are the most glaring design flaw in the human body. If mothers milk is too sweet it will rot them. In our cleverness we found the most delicious and pernicious diet that, amongst other things, requires constant attention to what is for most species a simple mastication device before the real digestion begins. We may be judged by the quality of our 'smile', that particular arrangement of teeth within the upper and lower jaw and how such is exposed by the curling of the lips. But from the standpoint of functional integrity, teeth bite.

Xmas

For as long as I can remember, we had trains at Christmas. Everybody did. In some ways it was a status symbol in that some families had very big trains, those giant Lionels with three rails and the turning radius of a car. A typical layout would take up most of the basement and represent a rail system that, to scale, would have picked up a load of cattle or kegs at the depot and rush them to market approximately 200 feet down the line. We had the American Flyer layout, cheaper to be sure, but smaller gauge and therefor able to represent a more teeming metropolis in equivalent area. In the early days we would set up a simple ring-around-the-tree-tinsel-short-fire-potential-catastophe like everybody else. Then I claimed a significant part of the basement without complaint and from that point on the trains, the little plastic houses and stores lit up with the old fashioned giant Xmas bulbs, the lichen shrubbery and the styrosnow, the paper mache mountain because there had to be a tunnel- that was Christmas to me. That might also be because of the year that my dad told me not to ask Baba what she got me for Christmas and I 'forgot' and asked her anyway and dad found out and made me spend the rest of the day upstairs in my room and all I remember from that year is hoping that my blubbering through the bannisters at the top of the stairs would get me paroled in time to enjoy a little shred of the waning holiday. It didn't.

Yes, there was a time when I viewed Christmas through the same blissfully jaundiced eye as any other tot who was looking for a good reason to remember why Jesus did this that or the other. I was electrified by the St. Nick myth as any other naif who stared out the window until... well, there was no clock, but at least one year I stayed up until I thought it was dawn and rushed downstairs to rip open the gaily wrapped packages whose contents I don't recall. I do recall that dad was royally pissed because he probably had only gotten to sleep a few hours before. I think I stopped believing in Santa around then.

Screw Santa Claus. Why shouldn't kids know that their parents care enough to try and guarantee them one fucking happy day a year? Even if they do amscray with the money grandma gave them to buy you something cool because the gas man would have wished us a very scary Christmas unless he gets paid immediately. Somebody explain to me the long term benefit of perpetuating the idea that a stranger is more generous than your own family. Then again, there are a lot of questionably viable part-time jobs dependent on the impulse sales in the weeks leading up to the jolly day when it is revealed exactly how well your family and friends understand your tastes and needs.

Guitar

My dad had a dark old 6 string laying around the basement that he got during the war and which I'd never seen him play. When I was about five I got interested in it and would sit in the cellar sawing on it with a coat hangar like it was a cello. One day, assuming the strings were supposed to reflect some melody in my head, I tried to tune the corroding machines with a pair of pliers and snapped the headstock off which I of course got major shit for. A few years later my parents struck a deal with the local music store whereby you got a Korean made acoustic for 25 bucks if you signed on for a couple months lessons. Within a week I had picked out "The Christmas Song" by the Chipmunks which startled my parents and music teacher but nonetheless did not spare me the horror of 8 weeks of staring uncomprehending at black spots on ruled paper. I once thought I wanted to play the flute but couldn't get past the fingering. My unmusical sister June took clarinet lessons and I learned to play the verse of 'Two Strangers On the Shore' by Mr. Acker Bilk on it, which pleased my dad as greatly as he was ever pleased by my musical acumen. But guitar seemed to work for me. I played through the pained fingers until I had callouses, signifying how serious I was. I could pretty easily pick out tunes from the radio like "Walk Don't Run" and "I've Had It". At one point I even got the balls to ask if I could play Ricky Nelson's "Lonesome Town" for the kids at our weekly dance lesson/socialization experiment class. I remember a balled up paper napkin flying through the air and landing right in the hole of my guitar. Undeterred, I played on.

I have vivid recollections of 'playing' the piano in my grandmother's attic even before becoming interested in the guitar. In my own head I was expressing the most subtle and blissful emotions in great detail and with the most splendid technique that a preadolescent hand could bring to bear. I think it's the same sensation that every amateur guitar god experiences at the discovery of distortion, the effect that makes everything you play sound so damn heavy.

I guess it always was and probably will be music that defines my expression. It gave me a toehold on life and allowed me to justify my Bohemian inclinations. Being considered a musician is a special and difficult privilege to the extent that parents should rightly discourage their children from considering such an avocation. Who needs the competition?

Writing

My first voluntary writing was a vindictive act. Probably around fourth grade and an idea that Randy cooked up and I was immediately sold on. 'The Carden Dictionary' was the name of the publication, at a time when I barely knew what a dictionary was. I just can't imagine what the spelling must have been like. The subject of the work was our (pecker)wood shop teacher, Mr. Carden, and the object was to quote or misquote his various asinine homilies and non-sequiturs and develop parodies with accompanying illustrations, all hand assembled like an illuminated manuscript. We hated the guy because one minute he was putting you in the lumber closet ("In the back, boy!") and the next he was all puddled up reading some Arkie valentine to 'the little hound pup' and expecting all these pink piglet northeastern postwar row-house development first generation TV addicts to identify with a displaced coon-huntin' inbred itinerant woodcarver who's life's greatest achievement was in peril of being accidentally eclipsed should one of his students actually figure out how to whittle an ashtray. Thus is authority defined. Anyway, I've forgotten what I wrote and if Sothebys doesn't have the original manuscript... just as well.

My elementary (and perhaps my entire) school experience is now a distant fever dream. I recollect it so like torture that suitably reinforced, I would become the Weisenthal of postwar suburban diseducation and pointlessly persecute those whose crime was to be only slightly more ignorant but much bolder than I. One could claim permanent psychological scarring as evidenced by the recurring (thankfully not recent) nightmares of oneself (rat) standing in a stairwell (maze) in a state of hysteria because if you don't find your way into the proper educational chamber before the bell you get no cheese (cheese). Often one is naked as well. Then there is the volcano dream...

We are things that make things happen. Mike Cotten co-opted a sound sample of this fragment of brilliant thought from an unknown source that should bubble up regularly in the collective consciousness but has appeared thus far only on the Tubes swansong Love Bomb album. We're not supposed to be things that things happen to. We make things. We make things happen. One could assume that the universe conspires to deprive. Not so. The stupidity of others is a beacon on the rocks of disaster. Knowledge is conveyed despite the ignorance of the messenger. School sucks massively and yet I did learn how to write, if only out of vindictiveness.

Cornfield

If you can believe it, my elementary school principal was Mrs. Cornfield, which is kinda from the same farm as Ms. Crabapple. She was, in my prepubescent opinion, the epitome of evil and had little to no understanding of the young minds within her charge. She had that prim demeanor of a typecast prude and obviously considered herself an 'adult'- think Miss Hathaway of the Beverly Hillbillies. One day she came into our 4th grade class to deliver some diatribe that I'm sure not even the teacher understood. I had already been shuttled to the furthest reaches of the classroom but at some point I became my dad and let out a bellowing walrus yawn. She took this as an affront and the next thing I know I am dragging a trash can over every inch of the property picking up gum wrappers, sniveling and wondering what I did besides being bored with Mrs. Cornapple's pointless droning. As years passed, there would be many meetings with my parents in her office anent my behavior and my wasted potential blah blah blah. I'm not sure my parents liked her either because I never got a lecture afterward.

WTF? I am emulating my dad and get shit on for it. The world makes no sense. I cannot win. Is it a conspiracy? Do all these older people plan my downfall? Whenever they set a goal for me, am I a sucker for trying to achieve it? Are there any rules at all or is everyone just using the so-called rules to be a dick to me? Is there something in me that is so repugnant that I am not worth sympathy?

Sometimes it's hard not to take other peoples awful behavior personally, especially if you are subject to their seniority. You think adults should know better when dealing with you and your naïveté, but in your youth you don't yet realize that some people will never grow up, never stop harboring grudges from their own youth and will never stop looking for someone to get even with.

Vacation

When I was in 5th grade our dad took us out of school about a week early so we could go on a family driving vacation through New England to Castine in Maine. By now there are four kids in the family and how we all got into the Nash Rambler with luggage enough for 2 weeks was an amazing and foolhardy feat. Though I was glad to be out of school the long rides made me bored and carsick from the smell of the damp floor mixed with my dad's cigar ash. Our first stop was the Howe Caverns, which was fascinating enough, then we overnighted at a 'motor hotel' somewhere in Connecticut. My parents left us alone while they grocery shopped and things somehow went off the rails. First we got into a sand fight on the volleyball court and I managed to hit my brother in the eye, then I was running around with my head down and rammed my sister in the mouth, chipping a lower tooth. Needless to say, there was anger and frustration with me for the remainder of the trip so I kept my head low. Things calmed down when we got to Maine for a few days stay whereat I had something of a breakthrough when I discovered a piece of driftwood on the beach that my dad fell in love with and displayed in the house forever after. On Fathers Day as we were driving home we stopped in some coastal tourist town and I searched for something to win his favor, settling on a giant novelty cigar which he shook his head at and refused to smoke.

That vacation with my family is a soup of emotional memories- the thrill of seeing new places mixed with the fear of fucking up any moment and feeling like I might not have any control over myself or what might happen to me. I can't imagine the frustration my parents had at not being able to send me to my room because we were all in the same room, although they did come up with the clever solution of me wearing a paper bag over my head. Mostly I remember the great disappointment I felt when my dad refused to smoke the ridiculously fat 16" long novelty cigar I gave him, not realizing it was never meant to be smoked.

'Vacation' is a National Lampoon franchise that represents all the chaos that goes into a family driving holiday, with the significant difference being that the kids are somewhat normal and the dad is the one fucking up all the time. This is, of course, our weird predilection to make husbands look stupid, especially in TV commercials. You'd prefer to think of your dad as Liam Neeson who, no matter how many times you do something stupid to get yourself kidnapped, will move heaven and earth to rescue you. Also, he's divorced from your mom.

Hernia

I awoke late one night with a pain in my groin and since my mom was still up I told her about it and she inspected my privates and the next thing I know there I am in a hospital bed. The result of either, by my theory, trying to mow the dewy lawn with our crappy hand mower or trying to pedal my bike up a particularly steep hill within the same day (thus the confusion), resulted in the rupturing of my 'pelvic saddle' and the leaking of my intestines through it. It's called a hernia. Things got complicated (nutsack involvement) so surgery was called for. For some reason I woke up on the gurney being wheeled back from the operating theater which threw everyone into a panic, the solution to which was poking me in any vein they could find, first in my arms and then in my feet until I was awake enough to beg them to stop. Once I return home, I'm amazed at all the attention I get (except from dad) and do some productive things like read whole books. A couple weeks after surgery my aforementioned gonad container became inflamed and filled with fluid, which I was later to learn could have resulted in sterility, but which history has since refuted.

I have always hated needles which probably makes me part of a very large club. First, there is the piercing which is often painful and creepy and your natural instinct is to pull the damn thing out as one would if pierced by anything. But then the hypo gets down to business and I don't know if it's worse that it's squirting something into you like a viper or sucking something out like a vampire. One of the highlights of my life was getting my polio booster orally- thank you Dr. Sabin!

My general recommendation is to never go to the hospital. It's a place of chaos and guesswork and that's were all the sick people are. Ever seen an episode of House? Someday we will have toilets that are doctors and robot pills that clean up all the stuff we do to ourselves, but until then, do not hang out with sick people.

Neighbors

Westbrook Park was white. There was not even a brown or Asian family that I recall. There were a couple churches of various denominations and the biggest building in the neighborhood was the Catholic Cathedral. I don't ever remember seeing a synagogue so if there were any Jews they had to travel a ways. I don't remember socializing with our immediate neighbors, the ones we shared walls with, probably because they had no boys my age. There was a kid named Bruce who lived at the end of the row who liked to pick on me- likely my dad and his were using us in a proxy war because he would never do anything about it. Benny and Tommy Boomer lived a few doors up and we spent a lot of time together, especially around the holidays because they had a big train setup in the basement. Their grandfather lived with them and he was missing a thumb- claimed he had pulled it off after it broke and wouldn't heal. Further up the street were Billy and Bobby Hummel whose dad was on the same bowling team as mine. Billy and I got along pretty well but Bobby was more of an idol- old enough to have a gig in the summer as a guitar player and he had a real electric guitar which he kept under the living room sofa. I remember to this day first laying eyes on the gleaming, pristine sunburst Strat in its plush case and feeling almost light-headed. I had never beheld such a beautiful and fascinating object in my life. Someday, I thought, someday…

It's odd how little I knew about the majority of our neighbors, everyone in Westbrook Park being so densely packed and all. I had a paper route for a while and would sometimes be asked inside when I came around for payment. Otherwise, I didn't much care for going into strangers houses, seeing the unfamiliar knickknacks and smelling the unfamiliar odors. It didn't help when my mother arranged for me to visit a boy across the alley who never left his house. As it turned out, he was in an iron lung, a sight that gave me nightmares after that.

Most of us don't choose our neighbors. What we mostly have in common with them is caste, one's place in society. Similar economics, education, cultural consensus, sometimes color or religion- all factors assuming you are making a choice where to live. We get used to our neighbors, but still prefer our own knickknacks and the smell of our own house to anyone else's. To that extent we remain strangers to each other, even as we all have the same number of bedrooms and baths… why does it always smell like cabbage in here?

Bowling

My dad Harry was a bowler. It was not unusual for a goodly number of local men to be on a bowling team sponsored by their company or civic org or church or whatever. It was at least an excuse to have an evening away from the family and with the boys. I could depend on Friday like a Catholic kid could expect fish in the cafeteria. Sometime around 8 or 9 I would assume any spot in the living room I pleased (usually prone on the couch) and watch whatever I pleased (usually Twilight Zone and Zacherle) and doze off with no awareness of my dad having come home at all. I never witnessed the leagues in action and fantasized little about the game but for the time when I heard that my dad's team played against a team that included Chief Halftown, a local children's TV celebrity and maybe a real Native American. On occasion we would do the weekly shopping at a mall where my dad bowled with me, and where I would inevitably suck because of my weediness and he would work on his game. We didn't talk about anything during these sessions but, until my mom showed up with the groceries, that was the closest to industry standard bonding as my dad and I ever engaged in. By the time I was a teenager there was a brand new bowling alley in the neighborhood where I would occasionally bowl, but more often play the nickel pinball machines and cadge cigarettes from other teens and pretend to smoke them while never inhaling. Fortunately, I never had the money to buy my own and never developed the habit.

My dad was never ever considered a physical specimen and didn't consider himself in any way within such qualification. But to me, having witnessed so little of him 'in action', ie out of The Chair, he became something suddenly graceful and powerful when he flung his ball down the alley. Maybe The Honeymooners went bowling and I don't remember, but he seemed to be himself to me during these sessions and not an angry and frustrated Ralph Cramden.

Bowling is a real man's softball. It's pitching underhanded with a giant hardball. That said, the game accounted for much of the time my dad and I spent alone together, perhaps obsessing me later in life to the extent of seeking out every lowly alley in any lowly town I might find myself in, trying to squeeze a few frames out before soundcheck. Then you wake up the next day with what feels like a railroad spike in your butt cheek and your hand swollen up to the size of a catchers mitt.

Theremin

I heard that there was some interesting musical show going on at the Presbyterian church we 'attended' and since I was perpetually bored I took it up alone. The place was about half full and the altar was packed with tables covered in hand bells and glasses and other paraphernalia that I was unaccustomed to seeing in the church. A traveling preacher and his family proceeded to go through their musical paces and it was all pretty impressive, especially when the guy hauled out the Theremin, which is a singing radio you play by waving your hands in the air. Most people are familiar with the sound from science fiction and horror film soundtracks. I was so awestruck that when the end of the show came and he asked for surrenderees to Christ I took him up on it, thinking I'd become a member of some society of Theremin players in the process. As usual, I just wound up on my knees in the pastors office blubbering forgiveness from God for being born while Mr. Theremin egged me on. That experience quickly lost its glamour for me but the effect of the Theremin was indelible.

I believe I once experienced a miracle. I was on an excursion into the city with some of my peers and since I never had any money somebody was covering my subway fare, which was a quarter. At one point they decided to pull a 'joke' on me and refused to cover my fare home, leaving me stranded at the Broad Street station. I prayed for help, not able to bring myself to ask another human being for a quarter. I was leaning over a railing staring into the filth next to the toll booth and there, half buried was a 25 cent piece. I had been shown a miracle! I had also experienced the miracle of being screwed over by my so-called friends. What a day full of epiphanies.

I've never been comfortable with the idea of talking to God. All the Gods that I've been introduced to are extremely busy and know everything already. I can't conceive that I would be able to beseech any higher than some middleman in the grand hierarchy anyway, but since I'm not sure of his/her name I feel like I'm talking to the government. I think it's best to let God do all the talking and the rest of us strive to shut the hell up about God.

Pinball

I enjoyed the profitable pastime of trash-picking and every evening before trash day I would go from can to can up one side of the alley and down the other. I'd often find valuables such as old girlie magazines or discarded radios that I would 'unbuild' or boxes of offering envelopes from the Catholic church that would stress certain 'holy days'- Christ's Circumcision was my favorite. A guy up the street worked for a beer distributor and one time I found a box of pendulum motors in his trash, a kind of clock mechanism that ran on a C cell that would simply tick back and forth, probably with a picture of a beer attached to it. I got the school kids to pay me a quarter each. One night I was walking down the alley in a somewhat distant neighborhood when I espied a garage that was spilling out the door with equipment from a defunct delicatessen. I snuck inside and in the back were two pinball machines, presumably in working order. Suddenly my scavenging turned to plundering as over the next several nights I snuck back in and methodically dismantled the machines and secreted the contents back to my basement. The end result was the 'brain' of the pinball lying in parts on the basement floor- the stepping relays and flipper motors and digit counters and power supplies and the little solenoid that would make the 'knock' sound when you got a free game. None of it ever really worked together again.

I guess it's a bit strange to turn to crime simply out of curiosity. I never had a real plan to rebuild a pinball machine from the stolen parts once I realized I could never get the bulk of it disassembled. There must have been exhilaration at the possibility of getting caught, but I never got hooked on the adrenaline. If I had been arrested and grilled about my motive the best I could come up with would have been curiosity. How does this thing work? The Victor Frankenstein alibi.

Few people can say they've never committed a crime, never sped or jaywalked or littered. Never lifted a candy bar or comic book when they were a kid. Maybe at some point you are so poor and hungry and underemployed that you might resort to thievery, perhaps forgivable if you don't decide to make a lifestyle of it. Crimes and sins are not the same thing- crimes you pay for here and sins you pay for in the next life. While I got away with gutting a pinball machine, curiosity is mankind's original sin and for that I will likely suffer many afterlives.

Somehow I became the mascot of an older kid in the 'ritzier' part of the world on the other side of the elementary school. We had similar interests, like amateur fireworks that disturbed his neighbors and not mine. There was in his house, as not so much in mine, a lot of R&B music which made it an attractive place to hang out. We learned that there was a musical revue going on at the Tower Theater, which I had previously only known as a place to watch science fiction and horror double features. We witnessed a lot of the songs we heard on the radio delivered in a literally slick, as in hair pomade and sharkskin, salvo of live showbiz such as I had only seen on TV. For some reason I was fixated on the song Book Of Love so I was especially pumped for the Monotones' performance, having kind of ignored what a terrible name for a group that must have been. I was also impressed with the theatricality of Gene Chandler's regalia fueled performance of Duke Of Earl. After that signature experience I don't recall my 'big brother' and I doing anything more memorable.

Once in junior high school we got called to assembly in the gym and the strangest, hippest thing that ever happened in school occurred. We were told there would be a musical presentation, then out came... The Orlons! They did their hits Wah Watusi and South Street and Don't Hang Up, likely lip syncing to the records or singing over them because there was no band. I was dumbstruck by two things: first, when did the teachers become hip enough to know who The Orlons were and secondly, did anybody notice that they were black? Because there wasn't a single black kid in the school, maybe the whole township.

Philadelphia was always a music town and in the early 60s a lot of that was defined by Cameo-Parkway Records. They were essentially a factory for dance-craze hits, starting with Chubby Checker's international smash The Twist and wending through endless offspring variations and on to Watusis and Mashed Potatoes and Gravy on those mashed potatoes. One had to have a knack for all these steps, not to mention dance crazes from competing labels. Perhaps because of poor reviews of my particular variation of The Twist, I have sworn never to dance in public unless I get paid for it.

Fireworks

My fondest family outings were seeing the fireworks on 4th Of July. I was so into pyrotechnics that I began to study the chemistry and construction principles and even found a so-called pharmacy where I and likeminded kids could buy saltpeter (potassium nitrate), charcoal and sulfur- in fact, they would remind you if you forgot something. My friends and I did many dangerous things in our various experiments and somehow never got arrested or obliterated. Sure, a few burns, but that was because we never developed the skill to build something lethal. One day a neighbor threw out a refrigerator box and I turned it into a 'fireworks outlet' by cutting two holes in the side and inserting cardboard tubes at opposite 45° angles. Kids would dump change in one and homemade firecrackers would come out the other. I learned so much that one year I went to the field where they were setting up the 4th display and impressed the crew to the point that I became a gofer all day and got to see the display from behind the line. They would have been sued if anything had happened to me. As a memento I collected large chunks of burnt-smelling paper and cardboard that fell out of the sky for further study. The next year I tried to volunteer again. When I got home after the setup my dad found an excuse to send me to my room from wherein I only caught the occasional rumble and dim light of the display. My dad sometimes enjoyed ruining things for me, especially if it involved me enjoying myself.

I've always loved the visceral aspects of fireworks and how they return me to a rare state of childhood bliss. The colors, the noise, the smell. And the danger, the possibility of fire raining down on you, your 'oooh's turning into 'yaaah!'s. The giddiness when you are making them or setting them up at the possibility you might get exploded. But the hypnotic, transportive quality of the intensely colored fire reminds you of something spiritual and primal and it makes you ignore the danger while it draws you in and makes you forget yourself for a moment.

It is much more difficult nowadays to find a friendly 'drug store' that will sell a minor all the ingredients to make a potential bomb. Maybe in rural places where moonshine is produced. But inside most boys and many girls is at least a desire to see things blown up. Between hi res VR games and blockbuster movies you can explode the whole world using our most modern day weapon: pixels.

Lump

Randy, precocious as he was, began to express a teenage taste for violent confrontation, usually with inanimate objects since the consequences were less severe. He was the only kid in the neighborhood who, not simply satisfied to own a .22 rifle, would take it out and brandish it like it was the best toy a boy could have. He bragged of shooting out streetlights over the park and I wasn't quite sophisticated enough to disbelieve him. Okay, maybe he did get one. He built a serious crossbow from scratch out of spring steel and walnut, babying every part and ensuring its power and accuracy by firing it into his bedroom walls and furniture. He once talked me into a gladiator battle under the footbridge in which I was armed with a length of 2 x 4 that had a circular saw blade slotted in the end while he had only a crudely honed 2 x 4 broadsword. He intimidated me with his aggressiveness (like I was going to hack him with a circular saw) to the point that he was unsatisfied with my performance and provided me with the additional advantage of a flaming rag on the end of the blade, after which I am so afraid of alighting one or both of us that he triumphs handily with nothing more than a piece of scrap wood. Then one day his mom gets a new dryer so we lug the old one out into the back drive and proceed to take turns pummeling it with a sledge hammer. We get a few good licks in and I maneuver around for a better angle, ignoring the fact that the back drive is usually used to dry clothes and there is a clothesline over my head. I take a mighty heave, hooking the hammer on the clothesline and from there it bounces off and onto my head. It's the only time I ever passed out.

By the time the hammer came down I was pretty used to getting hit in the head. I always thought that my jar was a bit protuberant to the point of distorting gravity in that any kid however lame who ever threw a rock at me from however far away would hit me in the head. Startling and painful as that is, never had it heretofore resulted in anything resembling a loss of consciousness, which must be serious but damned if I can remember.

There is today and forever a lump on my head from the hammer, a calcified hummock about the size of a dime under a little bald bit of forehead (now that my forehead has grown even larger). As time goes by it has a greater affect on my hairline in that no matter how I might prefer it to lie, a part wishes to form right along the piebald bit and, you see, there's this lump under it that stands in testament to the gravitational distorting abilities of my cranium and children will throw rocks at me or worse. You think this is a joke? Just wait.

Mall

Westbrook Park sprung up in a fairly rural area west of Philly so we had the opportunity to obliviously witness the evolution from country to suburb. There was the opening of our first fast food restaurant (drive thru!), a place called Gino's that was every bit as tacky as any McDonalds- given that there were no McDonalds yet. Just the whole idea of getting French fries and nothing else seemed revolutionary, the 15 cent cost suiting my budget perfectly. They built the Bazaar of All Nations on a swampy bit of frontage along the Springfield Pike, not too far from Randy's house. It was the first time we had seen or heard of a mall and it of course attracted us like rats, offering such strange new experiences as pretzel making and horseradish grinding and 3 for the price of 2 everything and being propositioned by pedophiles in the restrooms. The building was nothing so much as a long single story warehouse enclosing a quarter mile track of resizable stalls and florescent lighting. This monstrosity became the social hub of the surrounding communities and the place would come to an especial climax around the Christmas holidays because it was the cheapest place to buy equally cheap gifts. My family was sure to be the beneficiaries of the junk I purchased at the so-called 'auction' where everything started at $2 apiece and eventually wound up 3 for $2. A world of cheap clothes and appliances and watching bakers make cinnamon buns and Amish grinding horseradish and no black people except for the guy at the shoe repair cubicle, Ben.

Around the Christmas holidays the family would go downtown to Wanamaker's to watch the hourly holiday spectacle that was presented in the grand foyer at the center of the department store and featured one of the biggest pipe organs in the world. We never did a lot of shopping there because it was the most high-end store in the city and it looked it from the elaborate architecture and decorations. The Bazaar Of All Nations was more my speed, local and affordable and if it was tacky... I guess I never noticed.

There was a time when every imaginable item was available and deliverable to your abode through a miraculous device- it was called the Sears Catalog. For more than 100 years it was what the Internet is today. When young you would spend hours perusing the toy section in the back. When you were adolescent you graduated to the precursor of Internet porn, the lingerie pages. When you grow up you shop for tools and moccasins. Best of all, there were no popup ads.

Ben

Ben's avuncular attitude soon made him the attraction at the mall and I would hang around just to be in his aura of acceptance. He was in his late forties but had worked himself into a grandfatherly state, salt and pepper hair and a bit of a weary hobble. He was confident to the point that when I decided to test the tolerance of my parents by bringing him home (they passed with flying colors) and then my neighbors by bringing him to church (they failed miserably), he went along as an act of friendship to me. Eventually he saved enough to open a shop near his apartment in the black neighborhood of West Philadelphia. I followed him there, showing up on weekends to sweep his shop and go fetch BC headache powders from the drugstore. We'd go to gospel events (where, unlike the white evangelical analogues I had attended, nobody babbled in tongues and everybody testified in song) and eat in soul food restaurants and I didn't think much about the unusualness of our relationship. As time passed our thing cooled, me growing tired of the trek and he feeling more self conscious about the white kid tagging along in an all black world, sometimes evincing an unfamiliar exasperation with me. One day I realized we had lost our usefulness to each other and I stopped making the trip. I never saw Ben again.

On the way to Ben's shoe repair shop I had to pass stoops full of black kids about my own age. They always looked angry and would usually grow quiet when I passed. As petrified as I was I learned how to look like I belonged on that street and I guess that is supposed to be bravery. Was I afraid because they were black? I was afraid because they were adolescent boys like me and I knew what teenage boys were compelled to do to each other, to prove to each other. I was more afraid of the white bullies at school whose violent inclinations I was assured of. Perhaps it was the thought of racial consequences, that kept them from showing me the kind of abuse I might have experienced in white South Philly. If you want to make somebody a racist, hit them when they're a teenager and make them think the natural fear of their peers has something to do with their skin color.

Ben used to show me a pair of shoes he was making for his own young son who was living with his mother. They were a hideous angular construction that didn't even seem to permit normal walking, but it was a reflection of how specially he felt about his boy. I think I was the beneficiary of that feeling, that some of it could have been mine just by being around. And of course Ben was filling a void in me that my own dad neglected to even recognize. It is when you are separated that you realize the true object of your longing. For Ben, a son he could not bestow his love and attention on. For me, a father that did not know how to love.

Electronique

There was a movie that came out in 1956 called Forbidden Planet (that would have made me 8 at the time). Oddly, it was promoted by Quaker Oats which offered free tickets for kids under 12 accompanied by an adult so my dad took us young'ns to see it. I loved the movie viscerally because of two things: Robbie the Robot who became my hero and I was fixated on rebuilding him for myself, and the atonal soundtrack that was perhaps the first to use electronic music outside an experimental context. The former led me to learn about computers and the weird language of ones and naughts by which you communicated with them. The latter didn't manifest until much later when I found myself leafing through the bargain bin in the Bazaar Of All Nations record stall and happened on a psychedelic square foot of musique concréte and bought it on a 99 cent impulse. It came to represent another lobe in the small but genre sprawling collection of music that founded my world view of sound. The aural pastiches actually made sense to me, the dynamics and emotion were all there but the sounds didn't come from any instrument you could imagine. Most of the records were produced in Eastern Europe and the names of the composers would be something in unpronounceable Turkish. Over time similar records would appear in the same bin and I essentially cornered the market. Randy and I would have record duels trying to outdo each other in hipness and my EM collection became a regular part of the playlist alongside Carmina Burana and The Fugs.

I guess I always gravitate toward the less obvious. Why that is I can't fully or logically explain but it has been plainly demonstrated enough. How do you get equal enjoyment from Carl Orff and Tuli Kupferburg, though for different reasons? Senseless things are becoming the most important to me. I'm learning the entire Gilbert and Sullivan libretto not because there's a reward besides actually knowing it, but because it reminds me I'm not stupid and I can rise to a challenge. So long as that challenge has nothing to do with boring everyday school and the obvious things they want me to think.

It is theorized that music is man imitating the sound of nature, which is all well enough, but does not fully explain some of the weird music that man has come up with. Myself, I can't find anything natural in a country tune sung by a Yankee from a suburb. But we acclimate and eventual gravitate to the music we experience in our formative years, whatever that turns out to be. Eventually you turn into your dad- 'That's not music! Back in my day we had real music'.

Money

Randy and I inevitably put a serious band together and decided the name should be 'Money'. Randy took his family's 18 speaker stereo console and rebuilt it into a rolling, plywood and naugahyde, all purpose amplification unit- everything but the drums went through it. He also built his own guitar from scratch, that being a doubly appropriate term as he encrusted the entire body with little hand cut squares of glass mirror which kept his hands constantly sliced up. Collie played an extremely rudimentary style of bass, the most expensive instrument in the band since it was purchased new. We started out doing a typical Northeastern pop band mix of R & B and English wanna-band with a little folk rock thrown in because it was easy to sing and cause we couldn't hold onto a drummer. Just as we were trying to learn Rubber Soul the Yardbirds released Shapes Of Things and the Stones had the first fuzz-tone driven #1 record with Satisfaction and everything began to change.

You always dream that the band you are in is the one that will make it. Especially if you are clueless about how the music business works. You have discipline-free rehearsals and play a few gigs for low expectation audiences and practice running away from groupies in your high heeled shoes (don't wanna fall like George did in Hard Day's Night) and imagine you might write some songs once you finally figure out how to write one song that doesn't die aborning and try to find clothes that look cool without you having to perform amateur surgery on them and of course, you grow your hair. The hair that the other kids in school will envy and deride now but would soon flaunt in their own parents horrified faces.

Before so-called Rock and Roll there were frontmen and sidemen. The trend prevailed until the domination of The Fab Four signified the necessity of remembering all the guy's names and developing and opinion about their musicianship ('Who is the best drummer in the world, Ringo or Dave Clark?'). Now people argue how much of a quorum of original members is required to even make the effort. But the evolution also allowed a lot of players who wouldn't qualify as frontmen to have their contributions considered integral. Sometimes to the point where the frontman has to pretend to be a sideman to get any attention. That's why you've never heard of John And The Quarrymen.

Blues

The poppie sound of the Beatles and their ilk was making way for a more rootsy oriented kind of band. Now we were trying to learn all this guitar oriented stuff that suited our meager singing abilities and soon we met a guy from the neighborhood named Rick Valente who not only unburdened us of the responsibility of fronting but could blow harp on I'm A Man better than Keith Relf. He was seriously into the blues and had a lot of records by real masters like Muddy Waters and Howlin' Wolf and a new record by a Chicago outfit called The Butterfield Blues Band, all of which we devoured. I became fixated upon the slide guitar as played by Mike Bloomfield and Jeff Beck, mistaking at first that it was a special kind of instrument (that looked remarkably like a Fender Telecaster) and later fashioning a narrow 3 string slide out of a pulley I found in a box of computer parts. We had a drummer named Spoons for a while and during our senior year played a mixture of blues and grungy rock at dances as far away as NJ and frat parties in Society Hill and Catholic hops in South Philly where the girls gagged you with their tongues and dry humped you until your crotch was raw before moving on to the next guy. I think we actually got pretty good by contemporary standards, but then school ended and so did the band.

Subconsciously I had somehow combined my interest in computers and music. If I had not been so curious about that box of computer parts that Randy's uncle gave him I might not have found the pulley from a card sorter that, once the flanges were filed off, would make the perfect slide for a player who didn't realize that most slide players use open tunings. Such is the makings of a 'style'.

In a post-Beatles world it may be more unusual for a baby-boomer-boy to have never been in a band, to have never owned an instrument even if you never learned to play it. At the very least you stood in front of a mirror in your secret room and wailed and windmilled with some phallic guitar prop. There was something wrong with you if you didn't envy the guys who managed to learn to start and end a song together to the adoration of the opposite sex.

Electricity

Shortly after I took possession of my mail order Radio Shack Asian import guitar I started answering ads in the paper for guitar players. I finally got a live audition with something that sounded like a real band and had to travel some distance on public transportation to the location which was in North Philadelphia. I suppose I thought that my gleaming new oddly-shaped pickup and switch festooned instrument would be enough to get me over what must have been a hugely disappointed first reaction to my appearance. I left gaining only a greater experience of how to get to the nether reaches of Philly and found myself a bit disconsolate in the 69th St. Terminal waiting for the bus home. Two things happened to me (the sequence of which, I'm not sure of). One thing I'm sure happened: a guy came up to me and gave me an incredibly convincing story that involved his need to have my guitar and how he would get it back to me after he passed HIS audition and I somehow believed him and gave him the guitar which took 3 months to arrive from some Asian country and which has never been seen by me again. The second thing that happened, and you'll understand if I'm not sure when, is that I went over to a weighing machine in the terminal, an electronic one with a steel pedestal and that was supposed to have a glass face where the hype and results would be displayed but which happened to be smashed likely by vandals, and I stuck two fingers of my right hand into the empty maw wherein they touched the terminals that were supposed to power a light bulb and I was, to the surprise of apparently no one in the terminal, knocked on my ass.

Riding the bus home after nearly electrocuting myself, there was only one thing on my mind- I had nearly electrocuted myself. The fact that I had given my brand new guitar to a complete stranger based on a sob story never broached the visceral haze that lingered around my brain at the equivalent of discovering potential mortality for the first time. Sure, I had messed with a lot of dangerous chemicals but, struck by lightning...

Priorities are the most mutable thing in the world. One moment, the universe seems to revolve around tiny victories that settle small scores and soothe petty egos. Then you yourself are made small by a force of nature you may have been fortunate enough to have avoided but lurks out there waiting for the moment when you idly put your fingers on the electrodes and potentially stop your own heart. Guitar... what guitar?

Scouts

Because Randy joined the Boy Scouts I had to join the Boy Scouts. The meetings took place in the basement of the Presbyterian church once a week and involved not much more than keeping adolescents out of trouble. Randy advanced quickly through the hierarchy (Star, Life, Eagle Scout) so I felt obliged to make an effort by quickly accumulating the necessary merit badges to get to Star and become the leader of, seriously, the Beaver Patrol. This involved collecting coins, learning how to sew, and fingerprinting everyone in the family- yes, there was a fingerprinting merit badge. The troop had access to a campsite and once a month we camped over a weekend, summer or winter. We were expected to be able to pitch tents, start a fire with one match, cook our own food and sleep on the ground without freezing to death. Most of the Beavers were younger than me and I knew they were pretty incompetent so I did an excess of preparation for the campouts by making waxen fire starters and homemade MREs. Thus we became the pride of the troop. Other leaders had their own relationships. Carl, who was the first Eagle scout, apparently was caught bribing younger scouts with cookies to felate him in the warmth of the counselors' cabin. There was a drumming out ceremony where details were not discussed and Carl got bumped upstairs to Explorer. One time we hosted an inter-troop campout competition in which the home team did not fare so well, which pissed off the adult leaders no end. The Beavers were huddling around our fire in the final hour and somebody's dad came over and doused it with our drinking water out of spite. I called him a fucking something-or-other and that's when my scouting career ended.

I really did enjoy being in the Scouts. It got me out of the house, taught me something about leadership and gave me self confidence in the great outdoors. It made me join the church because you had to, but I can't say that I got the same lasting reward out of being sermonized while sitting in room full of people I knew to be hypocrites.

The irony of the Boy Scouts has been their historic denial of homosexuality when the reality is that probably millions of adolescents had their first homosexual experience with another scout. Yeah, there's never ever been homosexuality in the Boy Scouts like there's never ever been any in the military. The company of manly men.

Buttfuck

I met a professor during a camp counselor gig I took and he and his pretty wife made me feel welcome in their home near the U of P campus so I started showing up more often like a stray dog that knows there's a handout. He would alternately do his work and find records to play for me out of a vast collection that lined the fine wooden shelves of the high ceilinged library. He had a much better HIFI than my dad and turned me on to a lot of jazz like Horace Silver and hardcore folk music like Tom Lehrer and I otherwise have no idea what I did in return to entertain him. One night I caught the subway to go for a visit, the first time I'd gone after dark and somehow I got turned around at the station and started heading north away from the campus and into a tenement neighborhood. A couple of brothers in big hats and long coats pass me and I stop them to ask directions. They fake me up to the corner like to show me something and then one of them pulls out a knife, lays the point against my gut and hisses for me to head into the alley. They back me into a doorway and I'm assuming they're going to rob me until the guy without the knife gets behind me and starts undoing his pants. They order me to drop 'em and I begin to whimper "Oh God" uncontrollably, having no other inkling how to negotiate my way out of this situation. A moment later someone sticks a head out of a doorway down the street and the two panic and run off. 'God' retreated back into the house, uninterested in the shivering near-rape victim in the alley. I also miraculously regained my sense of direction and hastily capered to the professors apartment where I made no mention then or since about the humiliating experience.

When Billy Mumi returned from space he formed a 'band' called Barnes & Barnes and had a cult hit called Fish Heads. That from the album Voobaha, which also contained a little ditty called Homophobic Dream #27. My mofriend Joel brought it to our attention one Labor Day celebration and it became anthemic, evolving from a irresistible lilt to an endless opportunity for stentorian and comradely song, a refrain who's meaning resonates long after the last note fades. All together now: "There's a penis in my butt, hurting me, hurting me, hurting me..."

I've never had or imagined having gay sex. I've had a lot of gay friends, some of whom have come on to me but it doesn't bother me when they do and they soon give up. I don't think somebody's gayness should make one uncomfortable. I think it makes some people uncomfortable because they imagine gay sex and find the concept perverse and subversive, but the solution is simple: stop imagining other peoples sex lives. In fact, stop imagining mine. Get your own goddam sex life!

Mental

Being in the Boy Scouts pretty much required you to go to church, which I hadn't done in years. The Sunday services were as unbearable as ever but there was a youth group of kids my age led by a taxi driver named Bill. His story was that of a typical down-and-outer until he became 'saved' watching Ben Hur, go figure. He would take a half dozen of us out crammed into his old car and sometimes just drive around laughing and talking teen stuff then sometimes he would take us down a country lane and turn the headlights off while we all screamed in terror then broke into relieved hysterics when they came back on just before we missed a tree. These excursions pretty much became the entirety of my social life and I attended "religiously". One time he took us to a revival meeting in a hall in the city where there was some pretty good singing and a guy who jumped up in the balcony and started screaming a bunch of gibberish that scared the piss out of us. 'Speaking in tongues' said Bill without further explanation. Never went to one of those again. Because he was such a great example of his faith Bill convinced me to experience some of his life of service so I wound up accompanying him on his rounds at the Norristown mental hospital and in homes nearby where patients had been released. On the ride up he talked about the symptoms patients had and the different drugs they took and what side effects those produced. We visited somebody in the hospital where you never knew what exactly had landed them there then we went to someones home that seemed like a regular family except for the one who was on a serious psychotropic drug regime.

I found it odd that none of the other youth group members participated in these excursions, not because they were 'fun' per se but because I thought I might be the least devout, almost never reading the Bible and being in the group either because my friend Randy sometimes participated or because I believed anything was better than being at home. I never set out to be a Samaritan or fulfill commandments. I was simply witnessing someone who had.

We have a poor history of dealing with mental illness. First, we hardly know what it is, we just know what behavior will get you institutionalized. Once in the booby hatch you become an object of experimentation until some treatment or drug makes you socially acceptable or at least manageable. The crazy is a defense against a reality the mind can't handle, but that's no different than a 'sane' person who gets away with a warped sense of reality because others find it convenient to let them. More often than not, the harmless go inside while the worst remain among us, operating our institutions.

Drank

In 1965 the only drug I was aware of was alcohol and it wasn't considered a drug then so you could say I wasn't aware of drugs at all. I'd read a little bit of fiction in which people took drugs- Last Exit To Brooklyn and other books you wouldn't have read unless they were nasty. My parents didn't drink or even keep anything in the house but I was of an age group that was supposed to suddenly develop an insatiable thirst for beer so it was expected that you'd run into a drunk sooner or later. One night I was walking home along the garages from Randy's house and I hear a moaning from somebody's cellar doorway. It's Rick and he is falling down plastered and blubbering that he has to go home to his creepy mother but he's too drunk. My first response was that he needed drugs to sober him up so I lugged him back to my house and made instant coffee so strong it should have made him puke up anything that hadn't gone into his bloodstream, all this in plain sight of my father who said nothing and whom I believe was actually amused. I packed him a thermos and walked him around the neighborhood until he thought he could make it home. That pretty much took the edge off of any attraction alcohol might have had for me.

From all the caricatures of drunks and the trouble they got into as represented by popular media, I had made the assumption that liquor more or less made you literally stupid and since being 'smart' was the only advantage in life I seemed to have, I had no intention of losing that. I may even have had some germinal sense of dignity and since I was apt to fuck up even as I had never drunk anything, I was pretty sure I would make an ass of myself or worse.

Obviously, alcohol in itself does not make you permanently stupid. Generations of Irish poets and playwrights have certainly underscored that. But there is a point in any metabolism when even the most disciplined tippler will become saturated to the point of behaving like an idiot. For some it may manifest as a lengthy episode of bad behavior which will leave bad feelings for days. For others it is an unexpected and precipitous plunge into unconsciousness in a compromising location. That will probably get you a penis drawn on your face in permanent marker.

Dinner

About a year before I left home we were all having dinner and my dad was letting me know what a disappointment I was when I suddenly got the balls to tell him what I thought of him as a father. That precipitated the Silent Year wherein we would exchange virtually no dialog. I had already spent so much time at Randy's house that I more or less stopped coming home and the distance between me and my dad, not to mention the rest of the family, became astronomical. I would nip into the house for the few things I might need then hied back the the swinging bachelor pad that was Club Read where we had the freedom to do all manner of boy things like entertain young women when we weren't masturbating to pictures of women and playing loud incompetent music and being cynical smartypants about everything and everybody and ironically never drinking or drugging or having a car. I showed up at school when I felt like it and nobody cared. I never ate another meal at home until I left.

It was easy for me to overlook all the things my father had done for me in a moment when all I could think about was how little actual affection he displayed, especially as I was entering my critical high school years. I forgot the Radio Shack kits we 'built' together (I mostly watched) or the go kart frame that he had made and painted for me at his plant (but that never took to the road because I couldn't afford an engine). It wasn't that the rest of the family was getting what I wasn't. His role model was a childless bus driver. But I was sick of feeling unwanted and at that moment I resolved that no child of mine would be an accident. I would want them to be. And they would know that.

Growing up in the era of black and white TV meant watching a lot of families that were way happier than yours and who never got angry at each other or thought corporal punishment was as effective as a good heart to heart. It's impossible to imagine Ricky Nelson bent over Ozzie's knee being thwacked with a neolite soled moccasin. And what the hell job did Ozzie have that rendered him so devoid of rage that he could not lay a hand to his little boys butt, even if only to prove that Harriet didn't wear the pants in the house?

Linda

Late in my senior year there was this really pretty, really stacked blond girl named Linda that I had a great longing, pointless crush upon. Through some temporary delusion of hers (probably because I was the only longhair in the school) it came that she took a fancy to me and we began to 'get to know each other'. By the time I made a serious move on her she already had a nickname ready for me that had something to do with a rabbit, which made me even more self conscious about my crooked and rotted teeth especially when I was kissing her and attempting to give or get the least little bit of tongue. We had occasional private moments in Randy's room or some other friends parents basement which involved a lot of hugging and kissing and her enduring at least a bit of my inevitable attempts at fondling. I was hugely proud that she was 'mine' and lived in a relatively blissful haze such as I had never known. The inevitable demise began when I took her home one time and her dad turned the garden hose on me. Not long afterward she informed me that she was forbidden to see me anymore and when I grilled her about her reaction it turned out she was kind of ambivalent. Man, did that suck. I continued to mope and mail-stalk her all through the next winter without a response or a glimpse of her. I even bought her a really hideous plaid pants suit for Christmas and hand delivered it to her house. The only person at home was her sister who politely invited me in and chatted me up for a while. I left a little later knowing I would never see Linda again.

Thirty years after I stopped dreaming of Linda I'm in a hotel room in Tulsa waiting for sound check and the phone rings. "Hi, this is Linda from high school. Do you remember me?" Her voice has an unromantic Philadelphia twang that I hadn't noticed before. She's got a few kids and is planning to come to the show, which is on a blocked off street under a superhighway. I tell her things are chaotic and maybe I'll look for her and purposefully don't plan anything. I know that seeing her now, seeing the future I once thought I wanted sketched in cold reality would probably be more depressing than satisfying. If she came, I never saw her. I did not even imagine her.

If you believe in karma, balance, cosmic justice, you might find relief in even the most distant and forgotten slights being equalized. Never to gloat, of course, but to be assured that the system works for you as much as against you. That isn't the point. It's better for me to always believe I was the loser in my first love affair. That conviction forced me to find a discipline in which to express my virgin heartbreak and begin to write actual songs with words and stuff. Otherwise, my musical career might have ended as a guitar hero who couldn't keep up with changing tastes and had to become an A & R man at an indie label for big hair bands and unable to have a relationship that wouldn't be considered abnormal in Bangkok. Shudder.

Cutex

Just before graduation my father made it known to me through channels that I would be getting a haircut. I had not even planned on going to graduation, having already weaseled out of my yearbook picture knowing it would only mean more hassle about my hair. Apparently somebody at the school had called wanting me to acknowledge the trouble they had taken to force me through the system by removing the only symbol I had struggled to hang on to during the entire ordeal. My dad, vindictive since the 'dinner table incident', was happy to force me to oblige through the intermediary of my mom. I took the buck-fifty she gave me and went to Randy's house and bribed his mom into waving the scissors around my head a few times which only pissed off my dad and got me a trip to the real barber shop whence I was duly shorn. I literally cried my almost 18 year old self to sleep that night. A few days later I went to the graduation which was held at the Tower Theater, the movie house where I saw my first rock and roll show. Fortunately nobody had to walk up in front of the class and get their diploma- they just came down the aisles and passed them out like hymn books. Despite my parents collusion to make me presentable, neither of them showed up. I went home and in a rage squirted cuticle remover cream all over the fine purple leather cover of my diploma which ate the dye away and left grey streaks and then I decided I might need it as my only source of ID and qualification for a job, should I apply for one, so I quelled myself.

I don't remember when I first started to dream of leaving home. I ran away a few times when I was younger but didn't have a plan and mostly came back before anyone noticed. By the time I reached my senior year I was scheming about living in a thicket behind the school partly to be free and partly to prove that I didn't need my family, imagining them actually missing me. As my eighteenth birthday approached it became a personal rite of passage that had nothing to do with my procreation. There was no doubt it had to be a clean break.

Had I been born in January my life would have turned out totally different. The rebirth that legal adulthood afforded me would have happened in the middle of the school year, in the dead of winter and without friends my age to lig off of. Unbeknownst to me, the combination of spite and freedom that signified my decommissioning from the institution mixed perfectly with the cultural milieu that would become known as The Summer of Love.

Splitsville

My final days in Westbrook Park turned out to be an abysmal bunch of loose ends to tie up if I was going to make a clean getaway. Had to make up trig, had to avoid eye contact with family members, had to turn 18 and register with the draft, had to have a grand plan besides splitting, which I didn't, trying to recover from the trauma of the stupid haircut my dad spitefully inflicted on me just to please the "educators" of... my hair? Randy was going to college across the state as soon as possible so he could get a head start on his medical career. My fabulous romance with Linda came to an abrupt and painful end. With my grades and the family's meager finances there was never any question of me going on to higher education and since my dad and I weren't speaking the subject never arose. There was nothing or no one left in my neighborhood that I was going to miss yet I did not know with assurety what I was going to do beside getting the hell out. I had been hanging at the music store on downtown Chestnut and met a smallish guy with a pudding bowl haircut named Joe who said he was a drummer and when he sat down and soloed for 5 minutes the entire store stopped to listen. This guy had obviously been professionally trained. We started meeting up at the store with some regularity and as graduation approached decided we would rendezvous in Ocean City and try to put a band together. Finally, I had a 'plan' even though by the time I left I didn't even own a guitar. The morning of my birthday, I slipped the fifty dollar bill Baba had sent me into the cover behind the stained diploma and along with a few other personal effects in tow, left home- get this- never to return.

I can only imagine the bouillabaisse of emotions my parents went through upon my dramatic departure from the family manor, from ennui thinking I'd be back any minute, to relief that I might not, to horror that they may have to identify me at the morgue in the not too distant future, then probably back to relief when I wasn't heard from. Maybe I was hoping they would make some demonstration of giving a shit but it wasn't too long before I didn't give a shit whether they did or not.

My advice to anyone with an unhappy upbringing: get over it. I could have spent the rest of my life blaming anything that didn't go my way on my parent's mistakes. Yeah, but one day they'll be gone and who are you going to blame then? Pretend it never happened, own your life and maybe someday you and your family can be friends, and maybe even learn to appreciate each other and, god forbear, learn to love each other. Ever the optimist.

Eighteen

On my eighteenth birthday I arose, removed the typewriter from its case, typed a cryptic farewell message on a playing card (can't remember which, but I might have gone so far as getting a new deck so I could use the Joker- very poignant/cryptic), placed my few belongings in the case, left the card by the front door and split. My first stop was the Selective Service office where all potential Nam fodder must register within 2 weeks of one's 18th birthday. I then took a bus from the 69th Street terminal to Ocean City NJ where I was supposed to meet up with Joe DiCarlo. I arrived in the late afternoon and began wandering the beaches and gathering spots looking for Joe, whom most people had never heard of. At some point I learned that he had been caught up in a sweep of a crashpad who's residents had stollen some park benches and stuff. His parents came and busted him out and were returning the next day for a hearing. I spent the night between a diner drinking acrid colic coffee and a flop somebody let me nod in. The next day I hung around the courthouse until Joe and his folks showed up. Everybody got fined about fifty bucks, including a friend of Joe's who had no money. I felt inexplicably sorry for the parentless bozo and gave him the fifty dollar bill from Baba that I had hidden behind my diploma in the Cutex scarred case. I never saw the guy again. I went 'home' to central New Jersey with Joe and his parents.

In the year before I left home I started keeping later hours, but I don't think I ever went 24 hours without sleep. Somehow it was drilled into me that to see the dawn from the other side represented a commandment to sleep, although I pushed the envelope with regularity and made up for it by napping in class. I would snooze so deeply in Problems of Democracy that when the bell rang my legs would often be asleep. I would bolt upright only to crash against an adjacent blackboard and slump to the floor, a routine which eventually no one took notice of.

For uncounted years I lived for the moment when I would wake up 18 and begin to lead my own life. I could have divorced my family anytime but it wouldn't have been 'legal' freedom and graduation was just before with my birthday so the symbolism of simultaneously kissing off the public school system sustained me through the encroaching realization that I would soon be officially alone. A complete unknown, no direction home, yada yada yada... Afraid? How dare I be afraid of the formless future I have vaguely envisioned investing my life in for so long? I'm more afraid to stay and confirm everyone's worst fears about my destiny or lack thereof. For the final time I am running away. I'd feel more confident about it if I just didn't have this cruddy haircut.

Woody's

I had never really experienced a strife free household such as Joe and his parents shared. They doted on him and he occupied a huge portion of their suburban ranch style home, his humongous red sparkle drum kit sprawling across the entire second floor. We didn't have much of a plan until we heard of a package concert playing at a nearby summer stock tent. The bill consisted of The Byrds (interested), Shadows Of Knight (more interested, but disappointed) and Woody's Truckstop, a band I was familiar with, having seen a picture in Time magazine of the lead guitar player posing with a speaker phone in a small article about how he had beat the system and got to keep his long hair because he was "in a band' and also he got straight As so a judge said he had to go to class by phone. They actually stole the show so Joe and I decided to catch their next gig which was at a place called The Artist Hut, not a hut but a basement that held about 80 people. The first set was serviceable, but apparently they were having trouble holding on to drummers. Joe asked to sit in and immediately electrified the place with his rudiments. Jamming broke out and by the time it was over the band was begging Joe to replace their temporary drummer, Tim Moore. Joe agreed on the condition that they also give me a job. This seemed to work for them since The Paul Butterfield Band was a big influence, my addition allowing the rhythm guitar player to front and play harp. The Truckstop was complete.

I realized and accepted when I joined the Truckstop that I was to be the Elvin Bishop of the band- integral to be sure, but even I wasn't positive what an Elvin solo sounded like. I started out resigned to playing rhythm but had one ace in the hole: that 3-string slide I had fashioned out of a pulley from an IBM card sorter. I made something of a mark with this, while it never occurred to me that I had integrated computers and music in 1966.

When you are white guys in a blues band the eternal question is whether you can actually have the blues. White people feel sad, but is that the same as The Blues? There is a difference between playing the blues, however convincingly, and having the blues. But assuming you are simultaneously suffering romantic problems, unemployment, substance abuse and general beat-downess, yeah, anybody can have The Blues.

Carson

After the gig where I got hired by Woody's, the new conglomeration wandered around the city solidifying the concept and feeling each other out and I began to develop a camaraderie with Carson The Bass Player. He was still going to school at the Philadelphia College of Art and his parents were underwriting his basement apartment on 13th Street. He was Christlike in his invitation to share his quarters, my alternative being to flop at Arthur Heller's apartment across the street, a kind of 24 hour salon of local personalities, and this marked the point at which I began to live amongst my peers. I would soon learn of the important points of local interest- the cheapest places to eat, the addresses where the hippies lived who didn't mind if you flopped there, the other music venues you could usually get into free because everyone knew you were in a local band, nay, the most important local band. Philadelphia would become My City, not the place I visited for a few hours before returning to the suburbs. And now I actually had a friend in this city, a fun and funny guy who's worst vice was an occasional beer or two at the bar on the corner. We got comfortable enough with each other that we might both be bedding girls at the same time and not miraculously both wind up with the crabs.

So here I am, substantially without material possessions, lying in bed for the first time since leaving home that feels like mine and have whatever I can negotiate from the guy across what is in reality a tiny room, and it is a moment so blissful that it is nearly blotted out from my consciousness. I'm finally in control of my life and I am still alive. All previous programming has been imaginary.

What may seem to the perpetrators as idle acts of charity, even diversions from an otherwise embarrassing or seemingly self-serving response may, lottery-like, create a moment of pregnant opportunity. Such decisions may also lead to protracted episodes of painful interaction, like if the guy you move in with is some kind of maniac. If I figure out the formula, I'll let you know. Lucky for me, Carson Van Osten, my first roommate, was really a saint.

Philly

The lineup of Woody's Truckstop represented no particular shared experience except that we were all white guys fascinated with black music. Alan Miller came with the assumption that there was genius at work since he had beaten the system at its own game so when he went off on what it meant to be truly bluesy we tended not to question it. Carson was finishing art college on his parent's dime and was the most naturally entertaining guy in the band and the only one who could actually do a reasonable take on a blues singer, a reflection of his talent as a mime rather than experience in the Delta tradition. Kenny Radeloff played a reasonably functional keyboard and spent most of the time wound up and on the move about something. He was the oldest and the overall direction of the band tended to revolve around him and his necessities and compulsions. His younger brother Bobby was the harp playing frontman. He was even-natured and comparatively level headed for all the good it did and never played or sang in a convincingly bluesy manner and never really needed to since our audiences were nearly exclusively white and well populated with female admirers of his bohunky studliness more than our authenticity. We rehearsed in the 2nd floor of a motorcycle repair shop across the street from a black bikers hangout and ate in the black pool hall a few doors away, usually the hot sausage sandwich. We were always tolerated and never hassled. Between the music we played and studied and the radios and jukeboxes of the neighborhood the stylistic milieu was more about Chicago and Memphis than Philadelphia, with bits of London smuggled in. There was a network of houses and floor-throughs occupied by fairly even distributions of permanent residents and fleeting transients. One nexus was on the third floor on Pine, a block from the cheap diner we frequented on Spruce Street. It was there I first met Paul Fishkin.

Although I was pretty familiar with downtown Philly, I really had no prior urban lifestyle experience. There was a whole subculture whose existence had eluded me but now included me. So many people to meet, so many locations to hang in or sleep at, so much music to hear. This is exactly the life I would have imagined for myself had I known it was there for me- I would have left high school years before.

In Buddhism we reincarnate into a world of suffering because of trishna, the 'thirst'. Souls crave corporal experience and eventually find their way back to the material world. We don't actually know what we want until we are in it and often don't know that we are in it- the best of all possible worlds. Then like all things, it passes. Get a big face full of it while it lasts.

Paramount

The Truckstop made regular pilgrimages to New York City to see music that wouldn't reach Philadelphia. One warm summer morning we piled into a borrowed pickup truck and windlashed our way 90 miles up the NJ Turnpike to see a Murray The K show at the Paramount theater. This was not a typical Murray show. Well, it was a bit typical in that it featured his big haired wife Jackie the K and her troupe of dancers sporadically appearing throughout the show in sparkly costumes sleepwalking through some lame cruise ship quality routine to the consternation of a hugely disinterested post-adolescent audience. The show was a grind since they turned the house over every 2 hours several times a day. Each act below the headliner got about 5 minutes, which was enough for 2 songs. Most were there to see the headliners, Mitch Ryder who'd had a recent string of hits, and Wilson Picket who was probably unfamiliar to a good part of the mostly white audience. Anyway, that much would have been a typical M the K show. That it featured bands with names like The Blues Magoos and The Blues Project, neither of which sounded the least bit bluesy, at least made Murray seem tuned in despite his wife's antics. What really made this an extraordinary event was that it featured the American premier of Cream and The Who.

Seeing two of your biggest influences at once onstage is a pretty stupefying experience when you are still wet behind the ears. We were intrigued when Cream came out like they had just been to the hairdressers, white boy 'fros all around. That had no effect on my adoration of especially Eric and I found the 2 song set unsatisfyingly brief. Although I had heard about the destruction that accompanied 'My Generation' to witness it onstage was another thing altogether. I realized that, unlike almost every other band, with The Who you couldn't figure out "who" to look at. Every member was a show unto himself and when they essentially destroyed themselves onstage (several times a day!) it made it impossible for any act to follow them. Wet behind the ears? We were just plain wet all over.

Despite seeing our heroes go through their paces, that was probably when things started to seriously diverge between me and the band. Everyone would soon turn their gaze to the West Coast, while mine was ever more firmly fixed across The Pond. I did not want to be a hippy. I wanted to be English. Ironically, I learned more about the roots of rock music and how it should be performed from The Who in 5 minutes than I had ever seen any white people stake a legitimate claim to that wasn't stolen directly from black music. This I could do.

Cambridge

Kenny Radeloff had to go back to college in the fall so the Truck-stop decamped the security of downtown Philly and followed him to Massachusetts. Most of us crashed at a pad in Boston for a couple nights before a more permanent location in Cambridge was located. We were about a block off Mass Ave and a half mile from Harvard. I hated it. We never had any gigs or food or comforts of any kind. The police were giant pricks who would blow a siren at you when you were crossing the street and laugh when you freaked. The weather was getting colder and I didn't have the clothes for it so I bought a barely adequate pea coat at a thrift store with money I must have borrowed from the hippie nurse in the house who had the only job. The food situation got so bad that we took turns shoplifting from the local markets. I was pretty timid and uncreative, my usual contribution being a tube of biscuits and a stick of butter. We had a new bass player named Creed who was Native American and he'd hit the gourmet shop and return with weird stuff like cans of venison and snails and lobster bisque. We got desperate toward the end of October and went out as college kids on Halloween with paper bags over our heads and claiming it was a fraternity initiation ritual. Obviously things were getting pretty desperate when you're living on Snickers and Mary Janes and I was overjoyed when the band decided to return to Philadelphia, just as the first snows of winter begin falling.

I remember being on the Mass Ave bridge over the Charles River staring into the water and wondering, what the fuck? Everything seemed to have been going well in Philly, gigs were paying better, girls were plentiful, we were local celebrities. Why was it so hard to connect with another city? We played so little that I wasn't sure we were ever any good. One thing I was pretty sure of- if it's possible for white people to have The Blues then I definitely have them which, should we ever have another gig, will pay off handsomely in the authenticity department.

We often go along with a bad idea because everyone else is going along. If Johnny jumped off the Empire State Building would you do it too? Well, if all my friends are gonna maybe I will. Perhaps your not the only one wondering if this is a good idea, but you don't want to be the one that sticks the needle in that balloon. We know what happens to balloons eventually: they either pop of their own accord, or the air slowly leaks out leaving you with nothing but a flimsy empty bladder. Maybe you should have popped it in the first place.

Cellos

As the spring of '67 rolled around things started to get extra weird with The Truckstop. The "West Coast Sound' was suddenly hip (not with me) and the band wanted to graduate to a new level of drug consumption, and I quote, "move to the country and get our heads together". I still had never smoked pot or had a beer so the antics of the band became almost confrontational. Carson never made the transition to Cambridge- he had more serious concerns graduating from PCA so his parents wouldn't disown him. I stuck it out for a while, but then they decided that Carson's replacement should be a cello prodigy who had no idea what a bass player was supposed to do so opted to play cello most of the time. Open minded as I am musically, I had to follow Carson to the door. That was when we got the idea to form our own band. We had no name at first, but knew we were not going to the country to drop and pretend we were the Grateful Frickin' Dead. We began to stalk and plunder other local bands for the remaining components of our 'supergroup', and because of the Truckstop's rep, broke up at least 2 bands. Thom Mooney was in a folk rock unit called The Munchkins, wherein he overplayed everything, which made him seem like Keith Moon out of context. Stewkey was seated playing a Wurlitzer in a band that was so recently formed that nobody remembers the name since he left almost after their debut. But at certain times he seemed to sound a lot like Lennon and he was suitably studly for a front man, so all we needed now was a name.

I must have been feeling pretty cocky after I left the Truckstop, because instead feeling sorry for myself, I immediately came up with a plan that also involved the ruination of a couple of other bands to achieve. It wasn't as if I had thought it through completely. After all, I hadn't written a single song yet. I guess I never realized I might not be the only insecure person in the room and everyone is just waiting for someone to make the first move.

Go west Mencken said. But of course he was not a musician. The music of the west is like the west- earthy and sentimental and disorganized and it appeals to the cowboy ethos. I grew up in the colonies. My musical leanings are eastern- London, 19th & early 20th century France and Germany. Africa, India and beyond. Broadway! And a little south- Memphis, Mussel Shoals, Nawlins... Detroit, but certainly no further west than Chicago.

Nazz

The psychedelic revolution began to take its toll on the Truckstop just after the release of the Grateful Dead's first record. From then on it was about being in the head club and going to the country to get our musical trip together, a movement driven mostly by the band's more borderline personalities. Carson was summarily replaced by a cello prodigy (strings in the band- another loathsome West Coast influence) and I was still fired up about the Who and Cream so it wasn't long before I was gone. Since I was still sharing the basement with Carson, we began scheming and thinking up names and checking out the local bands for talent. Being in Woody's gave us the clout to lure players out of any of the mostly folk and blues rock experiments barely living off the club scene. Thom Mooney was in a band called the Munchkins who were pretty twee and lightweight so he was happy to leave for a situation where the drummer could go nuts. Stewkey was fronting an act that had been together about 2 weeks, sitting at a little Wurlitzer piano and moaning just like John Lennon which we thought might be doable since… hey, Beatlesque! We called ourselves The Nazz after a song on the B side of the Yardbirds 'Happenings Ten Years Time Ago'. We would be a cross between the Who and the Beatles, all harmonies and windmills. We became a local sensation. We immediately ruled a 20 square block area.

The Nazz was the first situation where I was actually in a leadership role. All of my previous experience as a troubled loner would not help me with the diplomatic and psychological nightmare of post-adolescent personality management. If I was to ever develop 'people skills' as such, it would be many years and many unpleasant studio experiences later. I suppose when you're that age you just get used to a certain amount of constant animosity.

When you have as yet no legacy, no body of work to empower your decisions, all you have to work with is your ego. In other words, people are just as impressed with your surety about what you can do as with what you've actually done. This handy realization has gotten me more mileage than my flimsy-to-nonexistent reputation could ever do. Regardless of my results, I have a high standard of accomplishments that I have yet to prove I can accomplish.

Kurland

We went to see The Who open for The Mamas & Papas at a venue near the U of P campus- a strange bill, especially as both acts were underpowered by the same pair of Shure Vocalmaster columns. After the show we learned, or deduced that the band was staying at the Holiday Inn downtown and sure enough, Thom Mooney and I found Roger Daltrey alone at the bar. We started fan-boying him and after a few minutes we were approached by a natty gentleman with an Oscar Wildeish aura who inquired if we were in a band. Since we went to great pains to always dress like we were in a band we were pleased to answer affirmatively. He asks us a little about the band, decides based on that and our looks that he would like to hear us play. The next day he brings an associate to our studio over the record store and we run through the few originals we have and a couple covers and after a bit of consultation with each other they announce they would like to manage The Nazz. His name is John Kurland and his associate is Michael Friedman. They negotiate a buyout with Jack and Jerry and soon we are bidding Philly adieu.

I'd witnessed enough 'a star is born' movie tropes to be skeptical of the idea that Flo Zeigfeld just happens to be in the audience the night the understudy takes the stage for the first time. We got 'discovered' and we weren't even doing anything except looking the part. Would everything that followed have never occurred, no Nazz records, no solo career, no beautiful women but for some skinny pants and a loud shirt?

I have probably always been self-conscious about my looks. But I have also always had a sense of what looks good, and fortunately grew into a body so archetypal that Granny's made suits from my patterns that exactly fit the mostly English pop-hipster types that shopped there. Thus I could take off the rack the most creative and outlandish everyday wear and with little effort assure my place as a fashionista. I suppose I just like to play dress-up.

LIRR

Kurland was ostensibly moving The Nazz to New York but finding a place in the city that had 4 bedrooms and rehearsal space was apparently prohibitive to we started looking for places on Long Island. Somehow we eventually wound up with a house on a residential street in Great Neck, the better part of an hour east of Manhattan. There was zero entertainment options in the 'hood so I found myself a regular passenger on the Long Island Railroad. Before the move I had never really spent more that a day or two in New York City and most of that had been in the Village in the neighborhood of the Cafe a Gogo. The uptown streets seemed incredibly wide to me- I had never really tried to imagine the scale of Manhattan. In fact, I had never been to Times Square which by the late 60s was in its seedy heyday. I would spend hours there at double features of movies I may have seen out of boredom or hope of some titillation, if you catch my drift. I learned at least small parts of the subway system, enough to to get up and down town. The management office was in an especially tony street where you might run into music and acting celebs going in or out of a house in the neighborhood. This represented the other perk of my city trips: access to the piles of promo records that came into what used to be a publicist's address. Who is this "Buffalo Springfield", this "Iron Butterfly", this "Vanilla Fudge"? Sometimes they'd show up days or weeks before official release so I had a heads up on the cool stuff. Some of it may even have influenced The Nazz. Then it would be time to get back to Grand Central for the long lonely ride home.

When I was very young I had a hard time sleeping because I didn't like being alone in the dark... who does? But as years wore on I found that I was quite happy with my own company and had no trouble entertaining myself. Early on it was apparent I had issues relating to 'normal' people so had few friends but for the occasional oddball. Once out in the world and away from school, it seemed the world was teeming with oddballs to befriend. Still I would always enjoy being alone as much as with friends.

The object of life is to learn to love yourself and the measure of that is how comfortable you are when alone. Yes, we are social animals but our initial instincts at an unfamiliar face are apprehension and fear, driving us inward. Can you hate yourself and still love anything else? Does somebody want to be loved by someone who can't be alone with themselves? Fear of solitude is fear of self.

Death

One day a call came in to the Great Neck house that John Kurland's wife, after entering the hospital a few days earlier, had suddenly died. Most of the guys were somewhat stunned, but had no immediate personal reaction beyond sympathy. I however, becoming attached to anyone who is ever nice to me, am overcome by some combination of shock, grief and disbelief, especially since no one thence known to me had ever died. I was already stifling tears as I rode the LIRR into the city with no expectation of what good it would do anyone. When I got to John's house Gloria Stavers and Danny Fields were already there, everyone trying to resolve the unexpected catastrophe and offer comfort. Kurland took me aside and furtively offered me his wife's wedding ring which I refused to take, being already weirded out enough.

It may be that some people will get through life without ever having been distraught, which I guess is distress taken to an extreme. The sudden death of someone I had interacted with just days before hit me like Buddha's first sight of a corpse. After a lifetime of depictions of death and fantasies of destruction, someone's unexpected passing was a distant rumble, not a nearby explosion. I had never imagined the effect of death on those still alive. Young and dumb and full of cum I didn't ever factor death as a possibility. Now the reality of it was on me like tar and feathers.

Why do we react so much differently to the death of a person than, say, a beloved pet? Maybe we don't, but you can't buy another Uncle Vanya like you can another Mr. Whiskers. It is one of the great aspects about our relationship with the animal kingdom that they will allow themselves to be anthropomorphized only to be supplanted in death by another similar, perhaps even more lovable item. NOTE: Ferrets do not qualify as legal house pets in many localities.

Eastman

The Nazz did a showcase or two at the old Cafe a GoGo which was quite a thrill for me and Carson having spent so many hours and so much of our hearing there only a few years ago. One night we were auditioning for Felix Papillardi, Cream's producer. I liked what he had done on a Youngbloods record and he wanted to work with us, but after I heard Disraeli Gears I thought the drums sounded wimpy so I changed my mind. Anyway, there was a freelance photographer at the gig taking pictures of the band and afterward she approached me about doing some shots with her in some other location. Her name was Linda Eastman and Kurland seemed to know who she was and thought it was ok so for the next week or so she would call me, suggest a location where I would meet her and she would take a few rolls and then we might go back to her house and eat chicken with her little girl. I was mildly attracted to her and flattered by the attention but although she had a superficial resemblance to my only high school heartthrob, her skinny legs and serious attitude turned me off a bit and I wasn't sure how I felt about doing it with a girl who already had a child. She did make me feel more comfortable with the camera and the friendship might have developed except she had to go to England at the end of the week and the next I hear of her she is dating then marrying Paul McCartney.

When I heard the news of Paul and Linda I felt a pang of envy and jealousy. Was I jealous of Paul for snagging a girl who had just weeks before spent an inordinate amount of time with me? Actually I was envious of Linda who now got to hang with the Beatles. How come she didn't call me and invite me over to party and sit in with the band? It could have been me up on the roof of Apple Studios grooving along with the boys on Get Back, blissfully unaware that these gods of all things good are about to hit the mattresses like a bunch of hillbillies, in large part over Linda and Yoko.

An argument could be made that the Beatles could not survive feminism. By the time the band began to penetrate the world consciousness, two members already had children, a third married within a year and the forth considered to be on the way to the altar. Yet this was so downplayed that (or so that) women of all ages could imagine the lads as still available. As powerful women replaced the invisible ones the focus drifted off the band and on to speculations of what would cause John to pull his little peepee out for all the world to see and why Paul's wife's New York lawyer family would be meddling in the affairs of the most sacred keepers of the musical grail. Feminism.

Being a publicist, John Kurland had distinct ideas about how to promote the band and had the connections to pull off his grand scheme. Even before our first record we were getting features in 16 Magazine, the premier music publication for adolescent girls. The editor, Gloria Stavers, was a good friend of Kurland's and would set up photo shoots designed to make us look cute and funny and already stars. Once she arranged for us to take over the hair salon at Henri Bendel on 57th Street for a shoot while we, especially myself tried not to look too uncomfortable while some stranger messed with my hair. We made sure that we were at any important events like a club opening or release party and always showed up in a limousine to the wide eyed whispering and pointing of the crowds who wondered who the hell we were. In between we would audition at every major label in NYC, usual an hour in the studio to record as many songs as we could perform live. Somehow the combination of bluffing and demoing finally paid off when Kurland got us signed for what he claimed was the largest advance ever for an unsigned band. The label turned out to be ColGems, a contraction of Columbia-Screen Gems, who's roster also included The Monkeys. Possible comparisons bothered us so they invented SGC Records-Screen Gems-Columbia. The best part of that arrangement was the distribution deal with Atlantic Records, which afforded the opportunity to meet and work with Ahmet Ertegun. A real legend.

It was a little weird, Kurland's theory of reverse success: get famous then do something to be famous for. Who knows, it might have worked out in the long run but it made it hard sometimes for the band to figure out its purpose. Are we players or pinups? And we kind of skipped the bonding that touring would have forced on us, not to mention the potential improvement in our performance. At least we still had the wardrobe.

"What's your advice for someone just starting out"? Do what you do. A painter paints, a dancer dances, a player plays. So often musicians claim to be waiting for a situation to arise before they get really serious. No point writing too much without that record deal. Don't want to play for less than 100 people. But no matter how much you woodshed you'll never know if you can affect somebody until you get out there and play for them. And if it turns out you suck, at least you can stop wasting your time.

Hollywood

We had an engineer named Chris Huston who was English and had been in a Liverpool band called The Undertakers. He had done some work in a studio in LA called ID Sound and the idea of going west appealed to us so to Hollywood we did hie for The Nazz first album. For some reason we thought that the producer had something to do with the ultimate sound quality and that the best sounding records were made in England so we tried but failed to get a British producer. Ultimately we made our choice based on the sound of a single song by The Shadows Of Knight, a cover version of Gloria. The producer was Bill Traut and he agreed to do the record, apparently in the old-fashioned way which involved little input about sound or performance and a lot of time reading the trades. Otherwise, the sessions were not much of an ordeal except for the budget-busting orchestral extravaganza I had planned for one of the songs. I didn't know much about scoring but it didn't stop me from painstakingly transcribing my ideas for 30-some pieces, to discover during the session that I occasionally wrote out of the ranges of particular instruments. Still, I got a lot of kudos from the players for attempting such a thing. But probably even more memorable than our sessions was the nights on the Sunset Strip. There was nothing in New York that so concentrated the ascendence of youth into a glowing snaking river of hair and glitter, music and sex and drugs, which we had no problem acclimating to. By the time we left we all thought we had girlfriends... and an album.

I had no prior point of reference the first time I experienced the West Coast and I was easily intoxicated by it. West was warm, East was cold. West was new, East was old. West was easy, East was hard. It wasn't as if I had lost my love of the Anglo-Saxon roots of Eastern white culture of which English boy bands represented the apotheosis. Even a whiff of such on me made the Hollywood girls swoon. I was a natural. What could possibly be better?

There wasn't a coherent musical scene in LA in the late 60's, and maybe there never was. You came to Hollywood to make movies, sometimes TV. Yeah, there was surf music and Phil Spector and what else? The Whiskey A GoGo was hosting mostly a stream of second wave English blues and electrified folk, the local talent mostly spent doing session work. It wouldn't be until Hair Metal and the Hollywood-style videos that promoted it that LA could claim a music movement of its own. Explosives and ingenues, right off the shelf.

Laura

I once visited someone who lived in an orthodox Jewish household where I discovered two interesting things: one was that I couldn't use certain plates for certain foods and the other was Laura Nyro's first album, Not Just Another New Sensation, which is an awful name for an album. There were some cool songs on it that a lot of people later covered like And When I Die and Wedding Bell Blues. It had an 'old fashioned' R&B/ Mann & Weill/ Goffin & King quality and something about her voice stuck in me, even though the music was nothing like what I was writing. A few months later her second album, Eli and the 13th Confession came out and when I heard it I was knocked completely on my ass. I fell in love with the record, I fell in love with her, and I started gravitating toward the piano as a compositional tool. Kurland knew who was handling her at Columbia (a former accountant named David Geffen) and through him arranged for me to meet her at her apartment. She was not as I imagined from her romantic album photo. She was heavyset with very dark eyebrows, dressed like a gypsy and spoke in a slow, breathy, nearly inaudible voice. She had nails so long they began to curl over and they made a clattering noise when she played the piano. She was still not 20 years old but came off as a slightly world-weary woman, having already experienced a ton of industry bullshit. Dinner was the only thing she knew how to make, tuna fish casserole, and I spent the evening in her aura and left dazed. A few weeks later she requested another visit from me, during which she asked if I would consider being her bandleader. I was flattered and shocked and although I knew I couldn't accept, considered the offer seriously anyway because of the proximity it offered. I never let the guys in the Nazz know what happened.

Though I had been devoted to other musicians through their recordings, I had never experienced the kind of crush that probably every adolescent girl has gone through a half dozen times- gazing at an album cover, listening to the music and feeling you are in the personal private presence of the singer. Though the people around me had no animus toward Laura Nyro, they had no comprehension of the space I was in either. That kind of 'yes, we understand each other even if no one else understands us' conviction that would melt under sober analysis. Despite my fanatic sobriety, such analysis was beyond me.

Laura Nyro and I were never meant for each other. She would become a mother, a feminist, a lesbian, a marginalized artist, a recluse, and finally a victim to a disease. Yet to this day my first experience of her most powerful musical expression remains as vivid as yesterdays epiphany.

Drafted

I was eventually forwarded the notice from the Selective Service that I was to appear for a physical at the Whitehall Street office in NYC. I had witnessed others in their preprocessing throes and since I was determined not to be drafted, sought to devise a strategy of my own. I didn't have time for Bobby's bananas and hysteria program and I guess I dithered around without an objective until the night before my performance. I went to Times Square and bought a ticket to an all-night film medley that I believe included Butch Cassidy And The Sundance Kid, but which I can't remember because of a self-encouraged delirium. I stumbled into the office around the prescribed time (probably should have been late, but I was still cowed by the specter of the 'government' tracking me down) and sat in a room too reminiscent of a high school POD class and was handed 2 subway tokens and instructed to fill out a test form. It did not take too much effort to flunk that and then we were whisked to the physical, the first event of which was the blood test. I hadn't thought much about this part, but as creeped as I was about the needles I kept dropping back in line until I was the only one left in the examining room. Figuring I had no recourse I scrunched my eyes as hard as I could and stuck out a skinny shimmying arm for puncture. The orderly refused to stab me, probably cause he couldn't even locate a vein and they sent me immediately to the shrink. It did not beggar his imagination to convince him I was gay as the day is long and procure myself the coveted 1Y designation, meaning I would not have to repeat my performance for a year.

Had I bothered to tally the number of friends and acquaintances that had actually been taken up during the draft I would have realized that all those war recruits had to be coming from outside my circle. I imagined them as the bullies I'd grown up around, scared but too full of bullying bullshit to come off as anything but glad to go. Twice I sat in rooms full of draftees who seemed no different in age and demeanor than the cast of Welcome Back Kotter. Young and cocky but not bloodthirsty. Not yet.

My aversion to military service could arguably be related to morality or cowardice, but the true explanation is much more direct and empirical: I am simply unsuited to taking instructions from authority. My entire life has been a testament to this behavior and it is my obligation to convince the recruiters of what a terrible pointless waste it would be of their valuable resources to try and conscript someone who will compulsively devote every waking moment to subverting authority. It's my patriotic duty to prevent such a travesty. We all do our part for the war effort.

Moogy

Many of my trips into Manhattan from Great Neck were for the purposes of hanging around the Cafe Au GoGo, and aside from getting good seats, possibly meeting some of the musicians or getting to learn something from watching a sound check. One afternoon I got to see Frank Zappa put The Mothers Of Invention through their rehearsal paces in an empty theater next door to the club. I met Moogy Klingman essentially doing the same thing- a couple of flies hovering around somebody's picnic. He played piano and ironically, grew up in Great Neck. He had a great interest in indigenous American music like blues and folk and jazz and the songs he wrote sounded like he came from someplace more colorful instead of growing up Jewish on Long Island. And he loved to jam. I found myself playing more with him than with The Nazz just for the fun of it. He introduced me to some of the very strange people he had grown up with, like Andy Kaufman before he started doing whatever that thing that he did was. Moogy also had a feral quality, like he had been raised by raccoons. It was very difficult to sit across from him during a meal as he tended to feed like a dog in a garbage can. And he was also quite unsubtle with women, seemingly not having the time to soften them up much before hitting hard on them, usually to no effect, which never seemed to bother or deter him. Somehow our personal quirks never erupted into anything serious and we exposed each other to unfamiliar artists and genres. We had fun.

When I met Moogy I was way more aware of other peoples behavioral quirks than of my own. I had a couple cultivated social habits like don't breath in somebody's face, try not to fart out loud, don't eat your boogers etc. I surely had not learned to control my tendency to blurt out my thoughts. In that regard I'm amazed that I got through life without getting my clock constantly cleaned. I guess I was also unaware of how much taller I had become since leaving school and that that may have been why I didn't spend more time with a fat lip.

Friendship is often depicted as some kind of Platonic love thing, but often you are not sure why you call somebody a friend. Perhaps it's common interests or aversions or 'friendly' competition but you rarely say that you fell in love with somebody without knowing it. Probably more friendships are based on mutual tolerance than anything else. Sometimes you just don't want to be alone and will put up with almost anything to avoid it, even while your friend is annoying the shit out of you.

London

We were all convinced that we had to record the second Nazz record in London. We rented a couple stories in the Queens Gate area near the Albert Hall with a veranda overlooking one of the city's many little gated verdant enclaves. The English autumn felt especially clammy to me so I backed really close to the 'heating device' until I smelt something like burning pants and Lo the back of my pants have been reduced to carbon. The grand plan is for us to record our Opus Grande at a brand new Trident Studio, which rhymes with Soho which is where the studio is and we're trying not to freak at how cool this is. I have declared myself producer which entails a bit of running up and down the stairs to the control room. We are so amped that we fire off a couple takes of Under The Ice and were pretty happy with the result. The next day we are served with papers from the British Musicians Union declaring we are blackballed from any union venue, studios included. We wind up spending 2 weeks shopping for clothes and sneaking in one press showcase at Ronnie Scott's, the general reaction being that we were loud. The best part of the trip was the coincident miracle that is Guy Fawkes Day. Every little shop on every corner was selling serious explosive devices and we made a pilgrimage to Hamlin's, the giant toy store near Oxford Circus where we bought the most beautiful and gigantic fireworks. We spent the holiday shooting things off our balcony and blowing stuff up in the street below, at one point we accidentally blew a passerby off his bicycle. At the airport on the way home I met Eric Clapton who remembered me from the Cafe au GoGo years earlier.

Whatever I had imagined about London, nothing in reality pleased me more than the discovery that in the weeks before Guy Fawkes Day anyone could walk into any little shop and walk out with a bagful of colorful and dangerous devices such as I had loved for as long as I can remember. Not puny little sparklers and flares but giant explosive conflagrations that could take your hand off or blind you. I was a kid again.

The 60s and 70s were a special time in London. It was acknowledged as the music and fashion center of the world. It was a concentration of culture so influential as to represent a new era of British colonialism pioneered by musicians but waged by Monty Python and The Prisoner and Richard Lester. O, to be in England... then came Margaret Thatcher.

Entropy

By the time we got to recording the second Nazz album I was getting pretty confident about the process so I declared myself producer which went down to mixed reviews. It was starting to become obvious that a band is not necessarily an exercise in democracy and factions are starting to form. Carson was laying low and Thom and Stewkey were tinkering with songwriting and I was being drawn into a balladic style by my fascination with Laura Nyro. The sessions were not completely joyless but there was growing indignation at my hogging all the composition to the point that the record swelled to a double album bloated with mopey songs that I sang in a flat style and that confused everybody. After it was mixed a consensus grew that the record should be pared back to a single LP, which angered me and pitted me against the rest of the band. It was during one of several heated conversations over the topic that Carson announced he was quitting. Once the fun went out of the band he began to yearn for his prior calling and leave music altogether to become a graphic artist. Kurland began playing both sides of the dispute and when he got caught I felt betrayed and quit the band as well. Ironically, Hello It's Me was taking off at radio. The band got a few gigs in far flung places and I would show up to collect a paycheck, never knowing who would be on the bass.

I had no plan B when The Nazz imploded. I had always planned for success. Maybe because we had always pretended we were already successful the hard work of achieving it wasn't what we were expecting. Somehow we lost the vision of what we were supposed to be. The fact that our management kept us off the road for so long in an attempt to drive up demand probably didn't help. We forgot what it was like to play together for an audience. The Beatles in reverse.

I and probably most everyone else bought into the idea that The Beatles were an ideal musical democracy. Their early movies never showed them in the process of writing or serious recording so it was assumed that if a song was credited Lennon/McCartney that they sat down together and started from scratch. We learned later that the credit was a convenience and most songs were owned by one and augmented by another. Or that the other guys rarely wrote as opposed to rarely being considered. That doesn't say as much about The Beatles as it does about democracy, a thing that rarely takes the shape we think it does.

Crows

After I quit the Nazz I couldn't stay in the Great Neck house with the guys anymore so I moved into an apartment on the Upper West Side that the publishing company kept for- well I'm not sure why they had all these apartments. Maybe for disenfranchised clients, as I was currently. I began to spend a lot of time commuting to the West Village to hang out with the Stone The Crows crowd, Andy and Marianne and Marty and a host of haberdashers and seamsters and nightclubbers and international players whom I met during a Nazz shopping spree at the boutique. Andy and Marianne had a flat that was a kind of tailoring commune, full of color and light and the smell of pane velvet being boiled in big pots to create the shiny crushed look that was a trademark of the brand. The milieu was distinctly Anglocentric (Marianne was distinctly British) and maybe more Bohemian than the hippie scene in that the Victorian morality was in total eclipse. Everybody did everybody and everybody was a sweetheart. Music played all the time and creative things were constantly materialized. It was cool. Somebody was opening a club under the boutique and I conned them into letting me design and fit the lighting which kept me afloat for a while and in the neighborhood. We'd spend nights at Steve Paul's The Scene because anyone who came to New York would show up and jam- Beck, Clapton, Hendrix- you never knew. One night I came back from the club with Marianne and a couple of the other sweet girls who regularly inhabited the workshop/crashpad and she concocted an orgy, which I shyly yet gleefully submitted to. Thankfully, little was expected of me.

I was crossing a horizon I did not know existed. Getting lucky? That was one girl putting out to you. I wasn't even getting much of that. But zero to three in sixty seconds? Performance be damned! Just the very realization made me reestimate myself. Maybe I shouldn't be so shy.

Right place, right time. It's not the same as fate, should you believe in such a thing. Fate befalls you, you don't see it coming, you resign yourself to it. Circumstance and opportunity. This what they teach you in the Boy Scouts: Be Prepared! But of course, the Scouts offer no merit badge in sexual confidence or pleasing your partner(s) should you find yourself in such an enviable circumstance. That would be the Playboy Adviser.

Grossman

Somehow Michael Friedman, having been impressed with my fearlessness of recording technology, tracked me down in the West Village and invited me to meet Albert Grossman. There seemed to be a hole to fill in their approach to making records and I was soon tested on a number of stable acts and newcomers. The first serious gamble they took on me was engineering Jesse Winchester, a draft avoider living in Canada. Robbie Robertson produced the record and other members of The Band did most of the accompaniment. I did my job well enough that I cemented my position with Grossman and got tapped to run the board for Stage Fright. Now that I had entered the circle, I was to learn that Albert saw himself as a man of elevated tastes and for whom a certain kind of excess was a badge of honor. He loved to regale visitors in the kitchen of his Bearsville house, slicing out some exotic cheese or cured sausage on the rustic counter that bore a tray full of two dozen mustards from around the world at one end and the entire country of India as represented by regional chutneys at the other. He drove a Land Rover before it was hip (or the least bit quiet and comfortable). He had a 10,000 gallon petroleum tank buried in his front yard. Everything he owned had a story behind it and a red insurance ID sticker somewhere on it. Within this enclave in the Catskills, he was King Of The Mountain.

John Kurland was kind of the popular image of what a showbiz manager would appear to be, dressy and imperious and in the model of Brian Epstein. Albert Grossman was nothing like that. He looked like Ben Franklin in baggy jeans and a buttonless Mexican peasant shirt. Still he was generous with me in the beginning, inviting me into his world. Of course I was of aware of the stories of how he would sue Bob Dylan year after year, usually over publishing royalties, but how was that to affect me at the time? I had yet to make a record of my own.

The music industry is full of legends about super-managers who might have only one important artist- Colonel Parker and Elvis, Brian Epstein and The Beatles, Peter Grant and Led Zeppelin. While Albert Grossman and Bob Dylan are sort of linked in that way, Albert went on to collect clients like he collected everything else, to excess. Like a collection of exotic condiments, some would get a lot of passing attention while others would sit unexploited, awaiting their moment. The upside is a certain freedom from scrutiny, which you might not get with a personal Svengali.

Home

Since I had been technically homeless since leaving the Nazz, the Grossman Agency put me on a salary and advanced me enough to get an apartment. I decided to look downtown but the West Village was as yet too dear for me so I found a nice sized floor-through on 13th Street off 3rd Avenue. The neighborhood seemed fine in the daytime, still sporting original brownstones, a small classic (porno) movie theater and the original Keihl's apothecary. I was to discover that a transformation occurred once darkness fell, what with screaming and gunshots and sirens at all hours. I didn't have very sophisticated taste in furnishings, tending toward bachelor pad accoutrements like patterned shag rugs and abstract prints and moderne seating options. Since I was not really a piano player and the place was not huge, I bought a little spinet that would follow me through several moves in the future. The back room was dark with no view so I pretty much left it empty and focussed all my interior design on the streetside room. Little by little I built my first nest, buying kitchen utensils I had never shopped for before, accumulating books and clothes and records, listening to music alone. Proximity to St. Mark's Place afforded regular diversion such as girl watching and 2nd Avenue was a bazaar of food options. The local diversions were no longer escapes from couches I was crashing on, I had a place to return to. Somehow, without thinking too much about it, I had arrived. Home.

I wish I could say there was a moment when I had the sudden realization that I had become stabilized, independent, unreliant for my survival on the charity of others. Since I had sworn never to show up empty-handed on my parents doorstep, things could have gone very wrong. I suppose in one sense I needed very little to survive and could have gone on mooching off friends or worse, strangers without missing what I never had, a space of my own. Now I am not sure how I survived so long without it.

Not everyone has the temperament to live alone. Tolerating oneself can be a surprisingly difficult thing. Learning to like yourself... Oy! Solitude is a commodity so rare that some people live in a form of poverty, a profound lack of peace and quiet. Home is often assumed to be where your loved ones are. For some it may be where everyone isn't. A place to be unconsciously yourself, walk around naked and talk to yourself, stop shaving and fart out loud. Home is where the fart is.

Max's

As crappy as the neighborhood was at 13th and 3rd, it was proximate to a lot of music venues like the Fillmore East and the Electric Circus and what became the ultimate post-gig hang, Max's Kansas City. It was a nightly ritual to amble over to Park Avenue, encamp in the back lounge, nosh on toasted chickpeas and kill a bottle of Bushmills with someone, usually Tony Sales, then somehow get home and wake up with no hangover. This was no soiree for the hoity toity monied crowd who frequented snobby, expensive 'discotheques' like Ondine. Nobody danced at Max's and if you wanted to eat you usually did it in the front room. The back was reserved for small melodramas and big personalities. There was the night Bebe made David Bowie cry or the night someone announced that they heard on the radio that the world was officially ending to little or no response. Things got pretty good when they opened a snug performance space upstairs where a I saw The Wailers before people knew how to pronounce Reggae, Steely Dan with the original lineup, and Iggy Pop diving on broken glass and coming up with shards stuck in his chest. Eventually a few more downtown music venues opened, most notably CBGB, but none had the back room where all the important hobnobbing took place. Eventually Glam lost steam and just a few years later Punk and Disco overtook everything and the idea of sitting around in a smoky room getting drunk gave way to snorting coke and moshing and the excesses of the latter 70s that made Max's scene seem quaint.

Max's was the first place where I was a 'regular', someone everyone recognized by face if not by name. I was miraculously in sync- I was a fixture at the place everyone had to be… though I might not have fit in at all but for the fact that Tony and Hunt's mom convinced me to try drinking, which I turned out to be pretty good at. And since I bought all my clothes in England I occupied a special station that few other denizens could manage- I was a New Yorker who looked like he was from London. The best of all possible worlds.

Any objective historian would have to admit that the 70's kicked every other 20th century decade's ass. It had everything: war, sex, drugs, prog rock and disco, stacks of Marshals and Max's Kansas City. Probably every era and every city had its must-hang for the intelligentsia, the artiste, the voyeur and the exhibitionist. Maybe there was an equivalent in every showbiz town in the 70s but this is, after all, New York Fucking City.

My first significant project for Grossman was engineering Jesse Winchester's debut record which was produced by Robbie Robertson and on which most of the rest of The Band participated. Things went well and I seemed to have a knack for mic placement so I was asked to engineer what would become Stage Fright. Bearsville Studios had yet to be completed so we set up the instruments on the stage of the Woodstock Playhouse and pulled all the equipment out of the remote truck and built a makeshift control room in the prop tent behind the theater. It was sweltering in the day and freezing at night and most of the time there was boredom waiting for a quorum to form and get in the mood for a few takes. There might be days when nothing would happen, like when Richard didn't show up for the session and was discovered with his car nose-down in a culvert. After the tracking we had to move the equipment into the freshly completed Bearsville Studio B so we did a couple days of overdubs in a studio in New York City, memorably W.S. Wolcott Medicine Show whereon I played baritone horn for the only time in my life. The Band had promised British producer/engineer Glyn Johns an opportunity to mix the album, as well as giving me a crack at it, so they sent me to England with the multi-tracks. We split the batch up and he mixed in one studio and I in another that I had never been in, then swapped reels. When I got back the Band was not satisfied with either version so we started mixing again in Studio B, the final release of Stage Fright being a combination of all three sessions.

There was a vast age and experience difference between me and the guys in The Band, exacerbated by the fact that I was a smartass with a short attention span. I may have been at several points in peril of being dismissed but for the fact that maybe I was the only one who was sure to show up when everyone agreed to show up even if I was the only one to show up.

Harry Smith, a musicologist that spent his life documenting the panorama of American roots music, was not himself a musician. He never had to deal with the quandary that Canadian influences represented. The irony of The Band was that Levon was the only American in the band. Somehow this naive klatsch of Canadians managed to reinvent themselves as Levon's neighbors, misdefining the American South as a place where slavery was an anecdote.

Scene

There was a club on 46th St. called 'Steve Paul's The Scene' which became a regular hangout for the Stone The Crows crowd. We were there pretty much nightly and the cavalcade of musical acts and after-hours jammers was truly mind boggling. The house band was The McCoys who always put on a good show but you otherwise might never know who would appear. I saw The Nice, Keith Emerson's original trio, who would play America from West Side Story while he physically abused his (Hammond) organ and threw knives at the back of it to simulate a gang fight. There was Tiny Tim before the Tonight Show, Sha Na Na before Woodstock and Alice Cooper before the makeup and wearing ill fitting costumes their moms had sewn for them. It was at The Scene that I first met Hunt and Tony Sales, sons of Soupy. They would mostly show up at the end of the evening when the jamming would start, waiting for someone to get tired of playing drums or bass. I also got into the jamming since I no longer had a band to play with and I held my own pretty well, except for the night Duane Allman showed up and wouldn't let a single other guitar player get a note in. One evening the boys invited me to come to their house on the upper west side next day and jam. They had studio set up on the top floor equipped with a giant double drum kit and two Marshall stacks. We deafened ourselves for an hour or so and for some reason the police never showed. That was the beginning of a checkered relationship.

I was never good at making friends with dour people. They often don't get the fact that I take so little seriously. The thing that attracted me about the Sales brothers, aside from the musicianship, was the sense of humor inherited from their father. Hunt was a talented mimic and Tony had a sarcastic streak so we hit it off well. Seeing humor in the same thing, like an obscure indie film called Putney Swope, bonds you like going to war together.

Some things are of an era. Clubs like The Scene and the Cafe a GoGo somehow survived on 2 shows a night for less than 200 people drinking ice cream floats out of flower vases so that minors could attend. Try to find something comparable anywhere in the world today- a place where real and often famous musicians play to exclusive audiences for pocket change or simply the fun of it.

Patti

I met Patti Smith for the first time at Steve Pauls flat on Gramercy Square. The McCoys had been the house band at Steve's 'The Scene' and Rick Derringer (I was just getting used to the change from Zerringer) lived down 13th Street about a block from me. Anyway, it was some kind of party and there was this skinny androgyne bobbing wide-eyed around the room and somehow we settled on the stairs and jabbered for a couple of hours, mostly making fun of shit in general and laughing at everyone else's expense. She told me she was working at a bookstore, grew up in New Jersey, that her brothers name was also Todd, and that she wrote and drew and occasionally read in public. We left the party together and walked around a bit. I don't recall that we did anything but talk, but somehow we must have arranged to connect later because I saw a lot of Patti for a while after that.

We were both skinny and androgynous and smart and outsiders and kind of perfect for each other at that moment. We were generous with each other as no one else was with us. I had no better friend. We saw the world through a common lens. We were still raw and street and yet evolving. An evolution that would eventually throw us into different orbits. But still we revolve around each other, even at a great distance and an astronomical pace.

It's not unusual to see a person for the first time and find their ephemeral presence a curiosity. Then they get stuck in your mind. Then, rarely, there is reciprocity and you get on each other's wavelength. I had never met a person like Patti, yet we seemed to have been the most natural friends.

Pot

I'm visiting Randy one night in his little apartment near the Jefferson Med School and he suggests we smoke some pot, which I have never done like I have never done any other drug. Since he's my best friend I can't refuse to let him pop my mind cherry so after many assurances I will not go insane I agree. At first it seems like I had smoked a ridiculous amount of product to no effect. Then after a while the TV seemed to be misbehaving... like maybe the sound as gone weird and out of sync with the picture, or maybe that's somebody in the room talking to me. The next thing I know we are laughing hysterically at nothing in particular and clawing at the TV screen imagining we had an effect on the blitherer thereon. I think I was sold. From thence I had to live something of a double life since I had been such a notorious teetotaler. I would only smoke covertly, even swearing Patti to secrecy as we got high together. It took me a while to come out of the closet, smoking mostly in front of strangers until I realized how stupid I was being.

My first stoned impression was that reality was a series of 3x5 cards and unless you were high, they went by so fast that they blended into a continuum. And while I still hadn't got control to the point of concentrating on a single card, there was an entire world in that snapshot. More than I had ever realized before. My mind was still running at normal speed, but I suddenly seemed able to have the time to notice details I had previously ignored. The world was new.

Sometimes you know you are going to experience something again as soon as you experience it. I wasn't sure why or what exactly I would get out of pot, but it was as if I had just learned to read. Some characterize this as discovering something hidden in the world, but I discovered how to read myself. I became an entertainment to me. I stopped taking everything so fucking seriously. And as a fringe benefit I became less of a social wet blanket

Fishkin

One of the first people I met in Philly was Paul Fishkin. He had a real place because he was supposed to be attending pharmacy school and then go into the family business but he became distracted by the downtown music scene and eventually wound up managing some local bands. After I started working at Grossman/Bearsville I began to look for a act to discover and Paul had a band he wanted to get signed called The American Dream so, voila- first and nearly last time I ever got an act signed. After the release of the record there wasn't much of a staff at the new label so Paul came to New York to sit in a room with nothing but a phone and pester program directors to add the single, mostly in vain. Everyone was so impressed with his perseverance that Albert offered him some sort of permanent position at Bearsville Records and since he had to relocate and since there was no one staying in the back part of my floor-through, I suddenly had a roommate. We were dispositionally compatible and Paul had almost no material possessions so the move took a matter of moments. Neither one of us was attached so we were a couple of lonely boys in the Big City. We had few social contacts so we spent many an evening cruising around the East Village hoping to make some connection to the opposite sex, never to any avail. Our escapades would become immortalized in song- We Gotta Get You A Woman.

I missed a lot during the production of the American Dream record. "Where were you when men first landed on the moon?"- in the studio with American Dream. "What do you remember from Woodstock?"- being in the studio mixing American Dream. All I do recall is a fight with the band over a toilet flush sound they wanted somewhere on the record and I didn't seem to take it seriously enough. That was my earth-shaking event of 1969.

The music business has its own particular ironies, stories of huge talents who never find an audience, spectacular failures that defy conventional wisdom, one-hit wonders who dominate then disappear. In some cases the personalities at the peripheries survive and thrive long after Elvis has left the building, Elvis for the purposes of this argument being a band that never gets to their second record.

Janis

Albert thought I'd amassed enough of a resume to take on a real challenge so he sent me off to Marin County to oversee album prep for his latest client, Janis Joplin. It wasn't an especially auspicious introduction to the Bay Area from my standpoint since I was ensconced in a roadside motel in Strawberry, a strip mall community between Sausalito and Mill Valley. Daily I would make my way to Janis' house where a cavalcade of songwriting suitors would pitch tunes to her when they could get her attention. Maybe day three and there are players and songsmiths waiting to present to her when I get a phone call from Janice saying she's at the police station and will be a couple hours late. Shortly thereafter someone accidentally leaves her bedroom door open revealing Janis still abed with a young partner and nowhere near the cop station. At some point during the process we get a call from Albert's office announcing that we will be recording a song no one has yet heard or approved and we will be executing it with the Butterfield Blues Band and we will do it in a union studio in LA whereat I will not be allowed to touch the board, much less tell the smartass guild member behind it how things should sound. Nobody has a lot of enthusiasm for the situation so it is no surprise when, after the union calls their first break we call the session off.

I was still pretty young and inexperienced when I got thrown into Janis Joplin's orbit, however briefly. I hadn't previously worked with someone who really had no interest in the process of making records. The live performance came so naturally that the details of making a record made everything seem tedious. I think Janis may have been happier if I had simply made all the decisions and just let her sing, but she was already a force unto herself.

What exactly does a record producer do? Before George Martin no one ever paid attention to producer credits. That recognition pushed the expectations of a producer into ever more peripatetic realms as shared only by quantum physicists and neurosurgeons. Silk purse to sow's ear? Easy. Capturing that flittering butterfly of musical genius? You're guess is as good as anyone's.

Critical

While I wasn't really more than a prospect in the biz, I did enjoy a pretty rich fashion life. I was living with clothiers and fashionistas and musicians, which seemed like counterculture. Patti had a whole other circle of artists and poets and authors who weren't as visible because they didn't dress up. She introduced me to her roommate Robert Mapplethorpe who seemed like an ordinary person who took photographs of people in odd circumstances. We went to parties primarily attended by minor lights and their groupies and aspiring authors moonlighting as rock critics. One night it turned out to be a lot of writers who were into music since Patti sidelined as a rock reviewer. Many would go on to start bands of their own like Lenny Kaye and Richard Meltzer and it seemed like a central concern was how to make rock criticism as relevant as rock music was supposed to be. I think the biggest difference between the writers and the rockers was the quality and of drugs available. I remember that the party ran out of pot pretty early and me and Patti and Richard wound up huffing a pile of stems and seeds burning on the windowsill. I think we may have started the fire.

I went to see Patti at a small venue one of the first times she did a solo show. She had a few little props, some books and a little portable record player. It didn't seem like she had an actual running order, or maybe she didn't rehearse it at all, but the performance was completely devoid of guile. It was maybe the only time I saw someone's aura when they were onstage. I don't know if anyone else saw it, but I'm sure I did.

It isn't necessary to be a musician to write about music, as it isn't necessary to be a musician to play it, which was the point of punk rock. But you will be confined to writing about the effect of it rather than it. This was the issue in the evolution of so-called rock criticism- you couldn't be more sophisticated than the subject you were writing about. Lester Bangs more or less defined the form: if you could not project your own anger and ignorance into the music it wasn't worth listening to. Unfortunately, that green lit every angry ignoramus to get into criticism, the end result being music that could no longer be criticized... Disco.

Alcohol

I was recording my first album and learning to drive like a maniac in LA while I was staying in the Sales family pool house in Beverly Hills. Soupy and his wife were 'estranged' so she essentially ran the household and because I was playing with Hunt and Tony I became something of a third son. When she learned one evening that I was over 18 and had never had alcohol she determined to get me drunk. Tony had passed that threshold, which was legal in New York, so he was allowed to participate in the ritual. It took quite a few shots (vodka probably) but eventually my liver gave up and shuttled the rest to my brain. At first I think I noticed the anesthetic effect more than anything else and was surprised that I could still form sentences and think kind of straight and apparently did not suddenly become Foster Brooks. There was a lot of giddy babbling but otherwise the evening ended without incident and I woke up next morning in the pool house with no discernible hangover. I would of course then turn to my friend Randy, who had a personal portable bar when he was 16, to see what he was recommending. From then on I was a Bushmill's Irish Whiskey man until I gained some appreciation for beer. Unfortunately, in later years I began also to gain an excess of liquid nutrition and had to buy new pants, banishing the spandex costumes to the closet.

It's hard to remember the first time you took a drug if you took it more than once. I remember the first time I inhaled nitrous and immediately realized I would not consciously do that again like I would never do DMT again because it felt like I was being smothered by Navajo blankets. Then there was that shoebox of peyote buttons I had one summer and that (hint hint) would make an ideal birthday gift even now.

You could say alcohol is a gateway drug except for the fact that in most cultures it's the only drug. The first time I got drunk was an initiation into a global culture I felt superior to simply because 'lips that touch wine will never touch mine'. That molecule and human history are inextricably entwined. One could spend a lifetime un-entwined. Guess I got entwined.

Putney

I was wandering through Manny's Music one day when suddenly... there it was in a glass case: the EMS VCS3 Putney Synthesiser (note the British spelling). I no sooner laid eyes on than it was in my apartment. Although I had seen and even touched a synth before I wasn't familiar with the underlying concepts so spent literally days under the spell of my new toy. I learned that you had to let it warm up for about 15 minutes after powering on or the oscillators wouldn't stay in tune and that you could plug a guitar into it and use the ring modulator to make weird sounds. I got pretty good at imitating the sounds of other instruments but the fun part was making noises that sounded like no instruments. Apparently Dave Gilmore from Pink Floyd came into Manny's looking for a VCS3 and I had the only one they stocked so they put us in touch and I spent an afternoon with him showing off what I had learned. By then I had also acquired the only accessory available, the Cricklewood Keyboard Controller, which made the box more than just a noisemaking machine. Soon there would be all-in-one keyboard synthesizers that wouldn't be as flexible, but would at least stay in tune. I owned a lot of them.

Though I was a quick learner in the studio and could be a bit creative with the technology, I didn't think of myself as 'cutting edge' until I bought my first synth. I was the only one I knew who had one, let alone knew how to make it work. As my recordings evolved the sounds of synthesis found their way into the projects to the point that people noticed and felt that the result was futuristic. I guess I might be more appropriately termed an 'early adopter'. I have a curiosity about new things even if I have no expertise.

Synthesizers were originally developed to make sounds that other instruments couldn't make and to some degree the history bears that out. Their ancestors were piles of wires and test equipment and practically no one tried to play melodies. With the advent of digital recording came samplers, those devices that can capture the original sound of an instrument and are technically not synthesizers, they are playback systems who's precursors were the Chamberlin and Mellotron, humongous mechanical monstrosities with tape loops connected to every key and that required constant maintenance. Nowadays, however you approach the sound it's all coming out of one microchip the size of a thumbnail.

Christine

I was in LA working on my second solo album and hanging out in a club when I was approached by a svelte girl dressed as if she was in a Dickens novel. She said her name was Miss Christine and she was in a girl group called the GTOs who had been produced by Frank Zappa. They were kind of proto-groupies (Miss Pamela later wrote a book about it) and Christine and I started going 'steady' and eventually she moved to the apartment in New York. It was the first time I had an actual live-in girlfriend, which took some adjustment, especially sharing the bathroom with all the makeup and stuff. It was a strange relationship, not a lot of 'I love yous' and such. We were mostly about dressing up and making the scene and having conventional sex. After a couple months she started disappearing for extended periods and would often get unusually cranky with me. One day I was in the bathroom and lying at the bottom of the trash can in plain sight were two used syringes. I confronted her about it and she admitted it was amphetamines, but otherwise took a blasé attitude as if it was no big deal. I made her promise to quit, but understood that she would probably just be more discrete so I wouldn't find out. That was the beginning of the end.

I have had an aversion to needles all my life and the idea of needing a drug so badly that you would perforate yourself regularly I find unimaginable. To discover you are living with someone who does so makes it hard to see them in the same light. They don't like themselves they way that you like them. You forget that it's their body to do with as they please, but you would never dream of poking holes in them the way they do to themselves. And often it's just to make their body feel good while they are destroying it.

Addiction is built in. Once we get used to something we don't want it to change. All you have to do is provide enough of it that you become accustomed to it being there, and while it's there you are not an addict. It's when it's taken away that you notice how much you need it, how much the other things you have don't matter. All you can think of is what you used to have. Sometimes it's drugs. Sometimes it's love. Sometimes it's Jesus. Waking up is withdrawal.

Canyon

Christine found a house in Nichols Canyon that had no architectural style to speak of and seemed far from everything. I freaked when I beheld it and was repulsed to the point that we never spent a night together there. My petulant plaints drove her back to San Pedro which pretty much signified the end of what had been a flimsy relationship. I resigned myself to living there and appointed it with an array of tasteless accoutrements such as a white shag rug, checkerboard coffee table, and the biggest waterbed I could find. I eventually adapted to it and incorporated it into the process of making Something/Anything. I rented an 8 track so I could record at home and life became a commute between ID sound and the faceless mini-mansion with breaks for food and occasional trips to venues that featured all I was interested in- music and girls.

I was finally getting a faceful of LA, that thing it seemed I had longed for since The Nazz stumbled into town, disappointed we were not in London. Still pretty much a sexual naif, I was stunned by the beauty, youth and promiscuity of the women. The faux British style I had assiduously cultivated was paying off in spades in the hinterlands. Crotchwise, my pistil is suddenly pollinating at a previously unimagined rate.

From the time we are born we are indoctrinated into our gender roles. Men are brash and predatory, women are demure and conniving. God help you if you don't get the distinction. But there are times when sex levels the field, roles are discarded and anything is possible. Androgenous pop stars suddenly get all the action, women are in full flower and intoxicate the atmosphere. We give ourselves away without guilt or shyness. We celebrate each other for what we are. Then we fuck it all up by falling in love.

Something

By the time I started my third album I was pretty much a routine pot smoker and the new vistas it provided manifested in a rising spike in my creativity. Although I hadn't intended a particularly unusual recording, the insights into the songwriting process triggered a barrage of inspiration and I found myself writing almost constantly, pulling ideas out of the air, tripping over new refrains at every turn. I would wake close to noon, get high, go to the studio (where I couldn't get too high or else I couldn't play), come home about 6 or 8 hours later, eat, get high, write and record some more and go to bed. I didn't go out, didn't watch TV, didn't have many visitors. It was the first time I played all the instruments myself so I was full of the challenge of thinking like a drummer or bass player. I had an 8 track machine brought in and would spend the evenings at home perfecting my synthesizer "chops" and doing Les Paul recording tricks and sonic gags a la Spike Jones. Randy gave me a drug he thought I would find useful called Ritalin and that became part of the routine as well, allowing me to bore deep into the work for hours on end. Rising up in the morning became rising in the afternoon. The record swelled to a double album who's only concept was prolixity. I pretty much had to force myself to stop.

It hadn't occurred to me at the time time, but at least the lyrical aspect of Something/Anything was mostly fueled by that brief relationship I had in my senior year. If there is a psychotropic aspect to Ritalin it didn't afford me the insight to realize the rut I was in. And while the music drew on a somewhat broader range of influences, even that was getting bit formulaic while still being dependent familiar forms. It was going to take a greater shock to the system to reveal what was really going on in my musical head.

Pop music is not about change. The effect of the ideal pop song is to make the listener feel upon the first listen like they have heard it before. This is not the product of calculation or computer programs could write pop hits (maybe they can by now). We are only comfortable listening to certain sounds and structures and culturally inherited modes, so when we write we gravitate toward the familiar, just as we listen. Then there are those rare instances that seem at first unfamiliar, even alien yet they dredge up something deeply primal in everyone who here's one. Thus Spake Zarathustra.

Quakers

The Something/Anything songspurt eventually began to slow down and I turned to creating some graphics for the cover. The day before I had to leave for New York I borrowed a camera and a light and set up a shot in my living room/studio that pretty much captured the essence of the monthlong creative marathon. I executed it as I had done my other work in the house, alone and to a satisfactory exhaustion and then I retired prepared to depart. About 5:30 in the morning I'm awakened by the sound of garbage trucks passing the house. The rumbling grows louder until I realize there are no garbage trucks. The earth under Northridge, California has split open.

I have had drugs that tried to destroy my consciousness and ego but nothing compares to having the surety of 'solid ground' so effectively nullified. This is something every animal cell in your body has grown to depend upon, the place you long to be when you hit clear air turbulence or find yourself puking over the railing into the roiling ocean. Suddenly there is no certitude of anything, no safety anywhere, no carefree comfort in the proximity of anything collapsible. It is The Big One. You know, the one where we all surf LA County out to sea and drown if we aren't crushed or swallowed up first. I couldn't stand to even feel the tremble of the aftershocks so I drove around in the rental until it was time for my flight. That day I thanked God when I was finally off the ground and into the turbulence.

I had to return to LA about a week after the '72 quake and learned what many of my generation learned in Viet Nam- the palpability of fear. The endless anxiety punctuated with flashes of terror at the slightest aftershock. The inability to completely loose the grip of a stalking death. which you imagine only as brutal. I eventually learned also that you cannot live by such fears, that you could suffer a pointless, violent or embarrassing death at any time and there are worse ways to go than at the hands of a powerful natural force. 25 years later at 4 in the morning I awoke to a similar earthquake in LA. I went back to sleep at 4:30.

Puppet

The first dog I ever had was a little black terrier LA stray the Hello People somehow inherited but didn't want to own. She took to me and Norman upgraded her from pup to Puppet whence I took ownership in the midst of making Something/Anything. She fit in immediately, especially when she displayed a propensity to get high with me by getting all licky up in my face as I exhaled a lungful of cannabis. This was a new responsibility for me but she made it as effortless as possible, seeming to approve of any idle attention without morphing into some cloying guilt machine. She was perhaps naive in the ways of the world, yet had an instinct for loyalty. I'm still talking about a dog here. I had never 'owned' an animal before and fortunately Puppet was low maintenance, never pooped in the house and wasn't at all picky about food. And what a party animal. One time I was walking her in NYC and she kept missing the curb and falling on her face and I started to think she was having a stroke or something. Got back to the apartment an discovered she had drunk a full glass of wine and was looking for more. I might have let her have it but obviously she couldn't hold her liquor.

My allergies to cats is a principle reason why I am a dog person, but certainly not the only one. Dogs like people and would like to be around them and protect them. Cats like to live in the alley and fuck the first pussy they smell. Even an untrained dog will warn you about strangers. Try to train a cat to do anything except, per the Mingus Method, shit in the toilet, which is no small accomplishment since cat shit is equivalent to nuclear waste. And I remember when a friend actually got Cat Scratch Fever and a lymph node in his armpit swelled to the size of a tennis ball and they had to stick a scalpel in it. What does a cat even do if you have no mice? Kill your parakeet.

There is the occult concept of animals as 'familiars', companions that can convey their special senses to someone they connect with. It's actually not that mystical. It's said that animals, even insects can sense impending earthquakes through subsonic precursors that humans have no awareness of. Or that some dogs can smell diseases on you, like cancer. Or sense your mood. And cats are notoriously spiteful, which beggars the question: Why a cat? And has there ever been a thing called Dog Scratch Fever?

LA-Hole

After I had kind of settled into Nichols Canyon, Patti came to visit me. Things abruptly of went off the rails at the airport when I made the erroneous assumption she had been there before, spent a while at the curb, had to go park and found her still at the gate. I raged at her like she should know better even though she had never been to LA before. Everything became strained from henceforth, even to the point of self consciousness over any physical contact. We couldn't do the things we would do in a normal city like walk around making fun of everything. This was LA- you drove everywhere. It wasn't long before she begged to return to NYC and I couldn't produce an argument to the contrary. After that there was a definite change in our relationship. We were still friends but we both knew I was the less dependable one.

It didn't take long for LA to have an effect on me and I think Patty saw it. I admired her a lot and wanted her approval, even as I was living in the tackiest circumstances, with the white shag rug and the bedroom-filling waterbed. I had yet to develop any significant empathy for others, even those I cared a lot about. I kind of treated my best friend like shit and didn't have the balls or brains to see what my new lifestyle had done to me.

NYC and LA may as well be two different countries. The natives of both cities assume they can survive in the other. But if you've never taken anything but public transportation and wake up in a place where you can't get anywhere without driving, or conversely, realize you are feeling castrated because owning a car is a luxury you can't afford... that is culture shock.

Marlene

After Miss Christine and I broke up I spent a lot of time looking at girls I thought I could never have, often at the Whiskey. They were, to a woman, nubile and in the flower of their youth and bra-less and the best reason for a young man to be alive. They all danced with each other for the benefit of the drooling male minority. One night I saw a girl dancing in a blue and white crocheted equivalent of a bikini with a smile that was perfect in its imperfection- a little gap in front like I had. I was smitten with her from that moment as I was surely convinced that I was not in her league. I became a regular, as she was a regular and one night she must have noticed my attention and approached me. I was mystified that she was un-attached and stupefied that she had an interest in me. We sleep together and I fall immediately in love with her. She is living at home in Chatsworth and part of my daily routine involves driving way out into the valley to pick her up and take her home. I write a song about her- Marlene. After a few weeks I have to do some business in England and ask if she will come with me. After a brief stop at the New York apartment we arrive at Gene and Marty's house on Shawfield Street in Chelsea. I am quite proud of my new girlfriend and chuffed that I can parade her around all the haunts I know like the Speakeasy and Harrods and the shops on the Kings Road, es-pecially Gene and Marty's shop, Granny Takes A Trip where I got most of my clothes. While I'm doing session work, Marlene goes out and explores the city. When it's time to return to LA, she says she wants to stay a little longer to explore some potential modeling gigs and figuring the boys would keep an eye on her. I get home and weeks pass with no word from her and she has moved out of the Shawfield house and no one knows where to. I am horrified that something has happened to her. Maybe more horrified at the possi-bility that she has left me.

In my young life I truly believed that this was the best thing that had ever happened to me. Why would such an ethereal creature express affection, possibly love for me if there was not something redeeming in me, something that overshadowed my shortcomings. That my adoration of her was not a vanity. I was not yet a success- I was still recording what would be my flagship album- so why would her feelings not be as strong as mine?

I never wrote another eponymical song to a girl after that, much to the chagrin of all the other girls who haven't already had songs writ-ten for them. Since the outcome was so bitter for me, it may have been that I had jinxed my own happiness by celebrating it in song. Haven't been willing to undertake that experiment.

Wisps

As soon as I got a break I returned to London to search for Marlene. That meant essentially hours of not knowing what to do between calling random numbers and processing rumors. Marty became visibly pissed at me for moping around Rue d' Shawville all day long, which was Marty who seemed to never have a steady but always have a girl. At one point I got an address and took a cab out to a remote dusky suburb and wandered around staring at any lit window in case she might appear, which she didn't and I wasn't about to go pounding on doors or going Kowalski and bellering her name all over the neighborhood. Miraculously I got a cab back to Chelsea. Whether it was my prowl through the neighborhood or the grapevine, a day or 2 later she called the flat and informed me without explanation of motive that she had 'moved on'. I do not recall if I had the pride to accept her pronouncement or broke down sobbing and begging, but I suspect it was more the latter. Ultimately I accepted the rejection and returned to New York.

During my hopeless search for the girl I had accidentally transplanted to London I tried hard to dull the ache. I must have drunk a lot but I don't remember being drunk. The only moments of solace I recall were lying by the front window smoking an uncharacteristically fat by English standards spliff and staring at the smoke as it slowly curled up to the ceiling. For a few seconds I was out of myself and in the world. Then anxiety, loss and guilt retook control.

There supposedly is a common wisdom about grief and stages you go through, yada yada yada. Problem is when you're not sure what you are grieving about. Is it the sudden death of a loved one or the sudden death of something that only lived in your head? The former is inexorable- they are not coming back. A dream was never real. How the hell do you bury it?

Brian

Something/Anything and the radio hits that it spawned opened a lot of doors for me. I got to meet Wolfman Jack and actually hang at his house in the Hollywood Hills where he phoned in his show while I lounged amidst the red crushed velvet and gold Mediterranean style everything. One day somebody contacted me to say that Brian Wilson had heard my record and wanted me to come visit him which I arranged to do. He wasn't huge or hairy or anything and he formed fairly comprehensible speech but he had the attention span of a chihuahua. He'd play about 15 seconds of a new Roy Wood single and then he'd be in the sandbox tinkling out some stream of musical consciousness I had trouble following. Then he gets it in his head that he wants to go out and I suggest the Troubador where Larry Coryel is playing. He's not sure who that is but he's game enough to try and drive the car which his helpers fortunately refuse to let him do. We're sitting in the celebrity box to the right of the stage and the demands of the guitar-driven 'jazz-rock' music are making Brian very agitated. A couple of times he gets up and approaches the bandstand only to return to his seat, much to the relief of his helpers. Suddenly in the middle of a long solo section by Larry, Brian jumps up onto the stage, grabs the mike and starts howling 'Bebop-a-Lula' in a totally different key and tempo. A startled Larry looks up to see Brian Wilson and begins to vamp with him for a while until the house security pulls him offstage and out into the street. By the time I catch up his friends have whisked him away. It'll be a few years before I see Brian again.

I've wondered since the Troubador incident whether the nature of the music had an effect on Brian's actions, if the same thing would have happened had Joni Mitchell been onstage, which I'd dearly like to have seen. I imagine the consequences could be far worse today if, say we had gone to see the Sex Pistols or Nine Inch Nails. Perhaps his behavior was actually a precursor to the blurring of the line between audience and performer that the punk movement engendered. Perhaps I had witnessed the birth of a revolution.

Brian Wilson did do something well before his time- he realized the potential of the studio itself as instrument and the possibilities of re-contextualized music, concepts that are very important to me today. So what if he talks out of the side of his mouth and gets a little antsy listening to fusion. Lots of people do.

Wolfman

The soundtrack of my year in LA was Wolfman Jack. This radio phenomenon was not illegally powerful enough to reach past Chicago so his, let's say, highly editorial (gonzo) style was unfamiliar to me. I was probably a laughable oldster when I moved to LA at 21 without a driver's license. After a couple of failures I got legal. Since you can't get from point A to point B without driving in LA, I ran through a series of rental cars, none of which were ever returned in original condition. But every one blared The Wolfman. When Something/ Anything became some sort of phenomenon, and also contained an eponymical tribute to a voice with no face, I actually got to meet the Wolf Himself. He lived up in the canyons behind the Beverly Hotel. He seemed little different from his radio persona, gravely voice, lupine mane, squinty one eye and all. We totally hit it off because we both liked weed. We dined at a too big table set with goldware (not just silverware!) in a room with red flocked wallpaper and talked nonsense and really warmed to each other. I kind of dug his over-the-top sense of opulence and once gifted him a silver goblet containing an ounce of the most primo herb I could find. Sometime later I retributed him with a song called 'You Cried Wolf'.

I admit I am hard to impress but I knew when I met The Wolfman I was in the presence of a legend. I found it ironic when years later he became more of a TV personality than a DJ and it kind of straight-jacketed him. The format didn't allow for the freewheeling rants and unexpected segues that defined his radio personality. Now everyone knew his face but not so much the performance that made him the howling renegade of the airwaves.

Media is measured in 'ages'. Styles of music and art that survive for more than a couple decades get their own era. The Age Of Radio outlasted a lot of other media movements. It continued to have great influence even after the onset of the Age Of Television. However, both would succumb to the Age Of The Internet, a medium which absorbed all others. Anyone could now be a DJ. So why aren't there those larger-than-life personalities like Wolfman Jack anymore? Because the internet is all about choice. Listeners no longer tune in to hear the snappy banter and inside jokes- hell, they barely focus on a whole song. Some service figures out your habits and suggests everything you hear. And if you don't care for it, skip to the next suggestion.

Nice

One summer day Gene got the idea we should drive from London to Nice and watch the Stones try to record. Gene was tight with Bobbie Keys, the band's saxophonist of choice, and thought we could crash with him. I was driving a rented Humber (which is nothing like a Hummer) that probably topped out around 50 mph. We took the ferry from Dover to Bologne and arrived in Paris by late afternoon. Gene had little experience of the city and I had none so we spent much of the time driving aimlessly around until dusk fell whence we moved on to Lyon where we snacked and napped in the car. Awaking with no sense of the route, we take what on the map appears to be the most direct path to the coast but find that we are touring the French Alps for most of the day. We finally reach Cannes by late afternoon and follow the coast to Nice, a half hour away. Gene somehow manages to guide us to Bobby's rented villa overlooking the Mediterranean where we snack again and collapse until the next day. We follow Bobby over to Keith's splendid house where a pattern that I later learn is typical is being played out, i.e. nobody is sure where anyone else is or when they might get around to doing something. By evening Gene and I have given up witnessing anything of cultural significance and head back to Bologne, this time driving an all night L-shaped route through Marseilles. By the time we get there it's 8 in the morning and we are out of gas and money and Gene has to call Marty to wire us the ferry fare. We kill time in a movie theater watching Return From The Planet of the Apes dubbed in French- very disconcerting to see the President of the US with that froggy sound coming out of his mouth. I think that was the first time I'd been to France. How romantic.

I was never as great a fan of the Stones as I was of the Beatles. I liked their early records but I thought they were growing gratuitous, like naughty middle-aging schoolboys seeing what they could get away with. I never imagined keeping up with the presumedly excessive consumption and therefor didn't feel like I could relate to them. Not getting to 'hang' with them didn't seem like a great loss except for how poorly our trip had been planned.

Commoners have the impression that musical royalty enjoy a life of endless creativity and spontaneity, struggling like Van Gogh (as played by Kirk Douglas) to reveal some fanatical, tortured inner fixation. Like Mick in the movie Performance, they leap into a St. Vitus dance of reflexive self expression, turning household objects into props at the drop of a hat and transmuting huge amounts of drugs into life affirming paeans of depth and imagination. And sometimes that's exactly what happens. "Take 37... let's try and make it look easy people!"

Badfinger

Apparently whatever talent I had as a producer somehow attracted the attention of Apple Records and suddenly I had the opportunity to be somewhere in the proximity of the Beatles orbit. Though I knew of Badfinger like everyone did from their hits Come And Get it and No Matter What, I was mystified at the opportunity because I thought they were already making progress radiowise and why did they need me? As it turned out I was the third producer to take on what had been a series of detours and false starts. An entire album had already been recorded and rejected by Apple and a second pass had been stalled when producer George Harrison became engrossed in the Bangladesh project. I certainly did not want to be the third producer to go down so I pretty much just took over the process, dictating what new material would be recorded, what would be salvaged and reworked and what would be tossed. There was not much objection from the band since the label had foisted me on them, likely with an ultimatum that something better come of it. The whole process was less than 2 weeks, whence I took the tapes back to Bearsville and mixed the result without input from anyone, label or band. Fortunately for all involved the label did accept the album and managed to break two top ten hits, so I figured the gamble had paid off and now I had a new reputation- The Fixer.

I had to admit to myself I was getting pretty good at this production thing. I was reaching a point where my experience allowed me to act with authority in the studio, to develop a philosophy about how records should be made and the success of the records reenforced that philosophy. Thus I could whip through a record in 'record' time, allowing me to move on to the next project and saving the label money in the process. Might I on occasion abuse that authority? Probably.

Artists and often producers themselves don't always understand the role one plays in the process. The producer does not work for the label or himself, he works for the artist. The artist ultimately pays the producer even if the label advanced the money. Artists misunderstand this when they feel like the producer is trying to make the record the label wants, and it must be explained to all that people don't buy a record because it's on a certain label. Producers misunderstand this when they think their reputation has anything to do with the success of the record because likewise, music is not bought because of who the producer was. The Artist will enjoy the glory or bear the scar of the final product.

Video

Since I had finally alit in a place of my own I could now enjoy many private hours of antenna-based video broadcasts, a media stream I hadn't previously deemed worthy of my anti-establishment world view, ergo I watched a lot of PBS which was starting to offer programming to independent public stations. I got hooked on The Electric Company because of the crazy things they did with letters and numbers and decided I had to learn a lot more about video. For one thing, it wasn't cheap to get into at the time. There was no such thing as a 'camcorder'- there was a camera, about the size of a cigar box, and a recorder, about the size of a cinder block. The most creative videography I (and most other aspiring video artistes) realized was by pointing the camera at a monitor to make swirly black and white feedback. The technology was moving on apace so soon I was able to afford a couple of color recorders and a variety of video synthesizers and manipulators. I learned about luminence keying and chroma keying where you can overlay images over other images and 'hide' the parts that are black or some particular color. I learned what the NTSC video standard was and that red looked the worst in it so you avoided using a lot of red. I started making music videos to Tomitas "Snowflakes Are Dancing" and other instrumental pieces. Video would eventually find its way into Utopia shows and TV appearances like Midnight Special. It was only the beginning.

I had a philosophy when I started making music videos that you would find a piece of music that was visually evocative and try to imagine it in video, which is why my early experiments all involved instrumental, usually classical music. I saw this as a new form of entertainment, even a high art. I'm pretty sure I'm not the only one with that attitude, but there weren't a lot of video artists overall since the technology was still pretty expensive. I was disappointed when 'music video' eventually came to mean a commercial for a pop act.

When most artists or musicians buy a big ticket item it's usually a foreign car or a boat or some other status item, which makes you wonder if there was ever a plan B. Occasionally, one has a dream of something they always wanted to do or learn about and the big ticket item can become a master chef's kitchen or college tuition or a workshop to build that car or boat in. Or some addiction like video equipment which will break you just as surely as an addiction to foreign cars.

Bebe

I had just gotten back from my Marlene ordeal in London when I found Paul entertaining a couple of attractive girls who he said were models and how am I to care being still too upset to even focus on a woman. A couple days later I'm moping in my bed and hear something pelting the window and see that it is one of the girls throwing pennies and I allow her to come up. Her attention distracts me from my misery and I am suddenly conversant again. She is very pretty and tall and willing and after a few days we are in bed. Her name was Bebe. She began to show up regularly and I began to surrender to her even as I had a hard time relating emotionally. Before I was aware of it she had more or less moved in without me actually inviting her. Her demure behavior soon gave way to a demanding and erratic personality, one that expected expressions of affection in exchange for sex and peace and soon I am saying I love someone that I'm not at all sure I can fully tolerate.

At a certain phase in a man's life his brain and his boner become of one mind. No matter how abused I had felt at the hands of a nubile sylph, I was suddenly eager for more abuse as long as my cock was involved. Bebe did not seem my type, especially in manner, but I guess I felt better about myself even after the awkwardness of the encounter.

Song Of The South was a feature length Disney live action/animation featuring Uncle Remus who recounts tales of Br'er Rabbit. One fable is that of The Tarbaby. Br'er Rabbit dresses up a big wad of tar in children's clothes in order to trick Br'er Fox and Br'er Bear into touching it. Once they do, they essentially wind up with tar all over themselves. It starts with only a finger, then a hand then eventually everywhere. The moral? Don't put your dick in a tarbaby.

Busted

Badfinger's second album seemed to have started normally, especially as we were scheduled to record entirely at Apple Studios. The first night's session was mostly getting set up and running a couple of the new tunes, wrapping up about 9 or 10. I walk the block over to Saville Row to where my car is parked and there is a bobbie inspecting it. Someone has apparently smashed the vent window on one side of the car, perhaps in an attempt to steal it. The rosy-faced young cop asks if this my car and I indicate it is. Before we get too into the details of what might have happened Pinky announces he is going to search me!?! It doesn't take the young zealot much effort to find the precisely 1.7 grams of pot on me and he arrests me on the spot. The station is at the end of the block so I agree not to escape and walk with the 'officer' wondering what the fuck just happened- someone tried to break into MY car and I am the one in custody. I'm sat at a desk and a frumpy detective out of Zed Cars comes in and sits on the edge of it and tries to convince me I am in big trouble and demanding where did I get the grass and when I've convinced him that didn't go to a local dealer for it (quite obviously the quality exceeded any you could find in England) then sent me off with a summons for a court date a few months later. Since I need to be able to enter England for work I flew back to appear in court, a fact that seemed to stun the bailiffs and such at the courthouse. While I was waiting in a white tiled room with the other cases I scanned the docket that was on a clipboard hanging on the wall- assault, domestic abuse, driving under the influence… and me, 1.7 grams of cannabis. When my case came up the only witness was the cop who arrested me. I was somewhat surprised, though I shouldn't have been, to hear the little swot lie his ass off to justify the arrest, claiming I was symptomatic because I 'looked pale' during the encounter- this from a guy with the complexion of a baby's ass. The judge made a crack about my income and I made a crack about British institutional drunkenness and was dismissed with a 25 pound fine and a future expungement if I sinned no more.

The hardest part of a government agent's job must be trying to keep a straight face while striving to intimidate someone over something like pot possession. You have either tried it and know how comparatively benign it is or you are already a regular user, probably from what you confiscate, or you are dreaming about the beer or cocktail you will enjoy when your shift ends. Power corrupts.

Here is a thing you should know about cops: they lie. It doesn't matter where in the world you encounter them. They don't arrest you to see you go free. They lie.

Candy

Bebe had a knack for coming up with drugs that looked like candy. There was a tiny pill that was supposed to be mescaline and later a larger pill that was supposed to be psilocybin and likely neither was either. She liked to get high, and god knows where the product came from, but It was a threat to my manhood not to ingest them gamely. The 'mescaline' trip was pretty fun- started out watching Valley Of The Dolls starring Patty Duke pretending to be on drugs just as the drug kicks in. Things became gooey and colorful and silly and so I committed to the 'psilocybin' the next weekend. This was not a gentle dissolution into an alternate reality but an unexpected skydiving event. I had to get out of the apartment thinking that stasis was death and we stumbled down what was formerly East 13th street but appeared to be more like the Grand Canyon. After what seemed like hours we arrived at Rick and Liz Derringer's apartment about a block and a half down the street. Since we had done a little tripping together before they indulged me and let me stand in the shower until I came down a bit. Then Rick played me the premixes of Edgar Winters new album that had Free Ride and Frankenstein on it and that's the last thing I remember from that evening.

'Why do people do this?', I found myself asking. You spend your whole life building a self image only to discover that it could be so quickly melted like butter in a microwave. The same dose seemed to have little effect on Bebe, as if her ego was made of Kryptonite or Adamantium. I was taking the trip personally. I felt challenged to defend myself up until the moment of surrender. As far as I could tell, she never surrendered.

Drugs are like a box of chocolates... you get the idea. Maybe the problem is when you decide that all you want is peanut clusters and throw the rest of the box away. Your life then revolves around peanut clusters. You do know exactly what you are going to get. You have no interest in anything else. Even after the clusters have lost their appeal, you haven't the imagination to see yourself enjoying a salted caramel.

I decided I should have a studio of my own and as it turned out Moogy had rented a place at 24th & 7th that fit the bill. 'Quad' was the new trend so I decided it should be set up for surround, although we made pretty much no quad recordings and soon discovered that the 4 speakers were too puny and opted for 2 larger Klipschorns. I built the console in a workshop at Gotham Audio, pulling preamps and pots off the shelves to add to the Penny & Giles faders I had ordered from England. All was installed in a desk I had made out of wood and covered in blue snakeskin Naugahyde. I was fixated with graphic equalizers, so the board had nothing but busses in it, no eq, and everything else was outboard with a graphic on every channel. The tape machine was a Stephens 16 track like I was used to using at ID Sound. I collected a few bizarre odds and ends like a Cooper Time Cube and a Pultec filter and set about to connecting it all together. One day I was in the second half of a psychedelic excursion and decided I should do some wiring, laying on my back for hours high as a kite and somehow getting most of it right. Days later I called the first session for AWATS before I had finished and found myself still wiring as the players were setting up. By some freaking miracle we now had our own studio and though it was a constant trial to keep it all working we were making real records. Secret Sound was a tres beaucoup atelier.

In 1972 most consoles were still custom made. I had been in many if not most of the major studios in New York and London and no two had the same desk. I certainly did have my own odd opinions about how things should work- I had never been in a control room where every channel had a 20 band graphic equalizer on it. I had always intended to make odd records and ignore the rules that most studios had to live by to stay in business. It would have been a waste of space and effort if the music that came out was simply conventional.

Technology is a lot like fashion. There is the latest "thing" and it's pretty expensive to get ahold of until the next "thing" comes along and then that other "thing" is suddenly cheaper. As time has passed recording technology has become so affordable that there is no excuse not to have it. That doesn't mean you still couldn't be talked into spending a fortune on the so-called "state-of-the-art" tech, even if it had minimal effect on the quality of your creative output. Neve and Focusrite are not going quietly into that good night.

Pre-Topia

I called up Tony and Hunt about an idea I had for a space-age concept band to be called Utopia. We would be super theatrical and have custom matching "space suits" and instruments. The tour would be the first to feature surround sound. And we would all have different colored hair. When they arrived at my door in New York from LA, Tony had day glo pink hair and Hunt had a reverse skunk, white on the sides and black down the middle. My French friend Jean Yves Labat aka M. Frog came on board to make synthy noises and process my guitar- obviously his hair was green. We auditioned a keyboard player from Gainesville name Dave Mason, who had to submit to an orange and purple dye job. And of course my hair was every damn color. We had a pod built that looked like a lunar excursion module with the green-haired alien inside and the drums on top. We moved the guts of a Hammond organ into a plexiglass case with a twenty pound acrylic diamond imbedded in the front. We had black body suits custom made by Norma Kamali. The show would begin 20 minutes before we hit the stage with what sounds like typical walk-in music which is eventually drowned out by the sound of a fleet of bombers approaching from the back of the hall and slowly looming overhead. On a cue there was a second of silence, then an atomic blast and a salvo of industrial-grade photo flash bulbs that was supposed to blind the audience while we took our places. We started with welding helmets on our heads so no one would see our hair until we removed them when the audiences eyes fully recovered. All this worked precisely once. After two weeks management came to the sensible conclusion that the tour was bleeding money and that was the end of that.

I must have had in my head some residual illusion about being in a band. The Beatles created the false impression that any collection of players could suddenly form a musical cooperative in which everyone was equal. That required me to ignore the fact that I had the idea, that I chose the personnel, that I was footing the bill to realize it. 'Twas nobody's fault but mine when it didn't succeed.

It used to be that everything was pass or fail. You were all in and if it didn't work you incinerated everything and started over. There was no such thing as beta, the not quite done version that you knew was going to fuck up at some point so you could find out what the flaws were and address them. Everything was hardware, carved in stone. The term software did not even exist. Now nothing is hard... firmware is as hard as we get.

Crowley

Despite having lived through the horror of 'losing' a previous girlfriend I had brought to England I took Bebe and our weird relationship to London. We were staying at the Chelsea Hotel (not in Chelsea, and no longer exists), in an attic apartment where I spent my days painting elaborate designs on my fingernails between shopping and actually doing my gig. Bebe did also her thing, which she claimed was modeling. One night I came back to an empty room that remained so until around noon next day, whence she reappeared spouting a most transparently unbelievable tale about "falling asleep" at Jimmy Page's house so deeply that she couldn't get to a phone. As I remember, I was unsympathetic. I see this as an opportunity to extricate myself from a relationship that hasn't been that great anyway, and then the begging starts. "Nothing happened", "I need you", "I love you". All pretty transparent, but for some reason I cannot resist the waterworks and actually believe this person needs me, and I probably felt empowered subconsciously and talked myself into thinking things would be different. I am a fool.

I'm thinking, does every girl I bring to London have to go missing? Am I simply an enabler for inbred English boys who are totally repugnant to English girls, but because of their accents seem to have some mystical power over young American women? That they play guitar and live in Crowley's castle and potentially bargain with the devil for certain secret chord combinations... is that why the fate of these fair maidens is inescapable? And worst of all, I had never considered fucking around on her. Who knows what kind of celebrity tail I could have denied partaking of?

At some point, someone discovers something you don't know about yourself. Like never knowing how much Jesus is in you until someone begs you to overlook the obvious and forgive the past and maybe the future. Suddenly you believe you could have such power, if only starting with one individual. Unfortunately, that individual may turn out to be Satan.

Nicky

I was contacted by a guy named Bruce McCauley about doing a short film based on the song Wolfman Jack. I had never been in a film before so I thought it would be a goof. We were to shoot my part at ID Sound (where the song had been originally recorded) so I arrived in LA a few days early to be fitted for a costume. Bruce rented a suite at the Chateau Marmont and while wardrobe may have been a factor, first priority was getting and staying high all the time. There were dick-sized oilers either afire or being rolled. There was cocaine which had little appeal for me, and opium with which I was as yet unfamiliar. And there was Nicky Nichols, to that date the most flamboyant gay person I had ever met, egging everyone to keep up with him. His modus operandi was to get 'inspired' for a real long time then get super coked up at the last minute and sew like a demon in the few remaining hours before deadline. For this particular shoot it was a silver lame jumpsuit with a neckline that plunged pretty much to my pubes which he gleefully fitted for maximum pudendal effect. During the shoot he made me up like an emaciated Gary Glitter and for added mystical appeal glued rhine-stones over my chakras, only problem there being that he ran out of eyelash cement on the throat chakra and substituted crazy glue for the rest which created water blisters down my chest from the stones I couldn't remove until after I had flown home and there remains little round scars to this day. That's how I met Nicky.

I was not to know at the time that I would soon become a canvas for Nicky Nichol's fantasies. Though I had figured out a look for myself, the idea of a personal costumer hadn't occurred to me. And while I was a willing mannequin the result did sometimes leave a trail of confusion, like when everyone thought I had come out of the closet on The Midnight Special because Nicky pasted feathers all over my face and flipped my hair like Mary Tyler Moore. Then again, it made me huge in Japan.

It's hard to argue that there isn't some relationship, even a symbiosis between genius and insanity. Maybe the correct term is more like 'abnormalcy' or 'exaggerated personality' but every once in a while you meet someone so crazy that the only thing that redeems them and keeps them from winding up destitute or institutionalized is some particular form of genius. It purchases the indulgence of others, either because they truly appreciate the gift or because they find the odd combination so entertaining.

Funk

Lynn Goldsmith had been photographing me with some regularity before she approached me about producing a record for Grand Funk Railroad. The band had just changed management and Lynn was designing their rollout as a 'updated' GFR which entailed amongst other details, finding a new producer. I knew the band by reputation, which was not particularly acclamation from a critical standpoint, but I was starting to enjoy the challenge of these kind of projects. Albert Grossman saw it as an opportunity to burnish his reputation (and mine) by demanding and getting what was the largest advance ever from a label for a producer. They had already decided on the album title and lead single, We're An American Band. I flew out to Michigan to meet the guys and hear their material and was pleasantly surprised at how open they were to input but also how much progress they were making in developing a more streamlined style of songwriting. It had been predetermined to do the recording in Miami at Criteria Studios. On the first day we set up and recorded the track for WAAB because the label had already set a release date for the single- approximately 10 days later. The second day we finished the overdubs, mixed the song and mastered it in the lab set up at Criteria. A week later we are still working on the record, but because advance orders could be counted as sales in those days the record had already charted in the top twenty- and most people had yet to hear it.

There are times in the studio when you think "this is too easy", that maybe good records are supposed to take a lot of time and effort. GFR was probably around when I realized how important the work you do outside the studio is. That more than anything people like a good song and if you go into the process confident you have a lot of good songs everything seems so much easier. More's the better if you can play with some expertise or personal style.

Historically, the division of labor in music has dictated that composers are not often performers and vice versa. Certainly most composers have learned to play an instrument, but the age of the 'singer-songwriter' is a relatively recent phenomenon. Used to be the troubadour was at the bottom of the musical food chain, a wandering minstrel. Now they are the gold standard of pop music, filling the odea that were formerly reserved for symphonies and operas, yea, selling out stadiums never meant for music.

Todd

Following AWATS was a daunting challenge but unfettered access to the studio revealed whole new vistas of musical tomfoolery. Our pool of musicians that came through was constantly expanding, many of whom were or were destined to be giants in their fields. We had plenty of great drummers so I could slack off that for a while and if there wasn't a drummer around we had these new rhythm machines that sounded quirky and cheesy which combined well with the increased use of synthesizers. For the most part I returned to a somewhat more trad songwriting structure, although marked by the same prolixity that blew my previous albums past the normal time constraints. I was not going to try to smush 2 albums into the space of one so I was soon working under the assumption this would be a double album. The most unusual thing that happened was the recording of Sons Of 1984. The concept was to teach two different live audiences the chorus to the song and somehow get them to sound like one choir. We put together a band (that would become the foundation of the second Utopia) and recorded the first audience at the Wolman Rink in New York City. And though there was much caterwauling from some very drunk fans, we actually got something of a performance. A few weeks later we 'overdubbed' an audience in San Francisco's Golden Gate Park, a group that was smaller but much more tuneful, as in less drunk. The end result confounded assumptions in that we had the East Coast on the right side of the mix, all rowdy and raucous, and the West Coast on the left side, ironically disciplined. The final package had one other unusual feature: Albert had suggested we put a postcard in the AWATS package and anyone returning the card would have their name somewhere on the Todd graphics. We got about 30,000 cards back and made a poster of my face out of all the names.

I realized my albums were becoming manifestos of a kind, that the only thing off-limits was convention. Through my constant production work I had become free of the economic pressures most artists felt when in the studio. My singular challenge was not to repeat myself, something that my peers were nearly obligated to do if they were going to hang onto the attention of a flighty and fickle audience that simultaneously considered change a kind of treason.

Most people, if they have a calling, will likely not realize what it is. Conformity is still the foundation of most societies and if your calling takes you too far out of the mainstream you are on shaky territory and nothing is guaranteed. But if you can succeed at it you'll find that many have tried and failed to survive on that barren plain and if you do survive you represent their hopes. Your calling is to hold that ground. You are the Individualist.

Re-Topia

After a couple projects and a live recording with a certain core of players I thought it might work to revive the Utopia concept. There was Moogy of course, John Siegler who had played bass on Hello It's Me, Ralph Schuckett who had been in a band with Carole King, Kevin Ellman had drummed for Bette Midler, and Jean Yves LaBatt aka M. Frog. Prog Rock was the flavor of the month and we were all itchin' to play some, me especially since much of my songwriting had migrated to the piano and I felt like I wasn't honing the guitar chops I had worked so hard to gain. Mahavishnu Orchestra was a revelation to us so we started composing long polymodal polyrhythmic marathons with bits of vocal and occasionally something that sounded like a song. When we hit the road after our first record the shows would last 4 or 5 hours, what with everyone taking a ten minute solo on every tune. I got Nicki Nichols to costume us, which most of the guys put up with without too much complaint. By the time we got to the second record Kevin had an opportunity to work his father's business so he was replaced by Willie Wilcox, who I met during Hall & Oates War Babies sessions. Roger Powell took over for M. Frog, who had done some interesting processing on my guitar during the shows but didn't really have the chops to keep up with the other keyboards. Now we had 3 keyboard solos every song. We decided to do the album live and recruited some background singers, one of which was a 280 pound Luther Vandross who wore a green suede fringed poncho all the time and during rehearsal in Bearsville would scream at any strange woodland noise because he was convinced real bears were going to attack him. Soon after Another Live Moogy and Ralph decided they wanted to do studio work instead and left the band. We continued as a quartet for awhile, then John decided he was done with the road. Before he left we got in one more project, a record called Disco Jets.

In Woody's Truck Stop and The Nazz I was not required to keep up with musicians of the caliber that comprised Utopia. We were comparing ourselves individually to our various heroes as well as to each other and I developed a whole new relationship with the guitar. The material was structured in a way that left long passages without vocals and an uninterrupted focus on the instrument. For fleeting moments I could channel the inner mounting flame.

There is an argument for never learning to read music, that being the resulting inability to play something that isn't written. There is nothing like the relationship with an instrument that is as fluid as speaking your mind. Now you just have to find something worth saying.

Dolls

I got an offer to produce a band called the New York Dolls who were pretty much the hottest thing in the so-called punk movement, which I'm not sure was called punk yet. We all used to hang around at Max's and though not formally introduced, knew each other by sight. I wasn't crazy about what seemed to be a homage to the Stones in drag but they were more exciting than the rest of the god-knows-what-in-drag bands that fleshed out the scene. I decided to do it because it was different and because I knew I was leaving New York City for greener pastures. David Johansen, the 'Mick Jagger' of the band, was the soberest and tried to keep everybody in line which compensated for the fact that he sang like an angry Louie Prima, which I imagine came in handier in the later Buster Poindexter years. Johnny Thunders, the 'Keith Richards' of the band, was working on a doctorate in sullenness which must have contributed greatly to his signature guitar style but may have been more fully represented in his hairstyle. The sessions turned out to be orgies of klingons and critics ecstatic at being close to a level of creativity they could finally understand and putting the band in the position of fulfilling everyones fantasy about having an American Stones on a Mercury Records budget. Miraculously they exerted the discipline to finish the record with all hands still alive only to rush the mixes so the band could make a club appearance and allowing the label to cut corners on the mastering. I guess no one realized that this would come to represent fully half of their total recorded output.

I remember going to see the Dolls at a beautiful venue in the Waldorf Astoria and they kicked serious ass. In point of fact I don't know if they played that well but the gig looked like a latter day Lenny Kravitz video fantasy, gilt and turquoise opera boxes and smoke and deafening noise and the as-yet-un-pierced pre-punk glam crowd rocking seriously out and I bet I was drunk. I did feel like I belonged to a special club having contributed to their unforeseeably brief fling.

John Lydon claims that the Sex Pistols were inspired by the Dolls who I know were inspired by the Stones who we all know were inspired by Muddy Waters and Howlin' Wolf and from there the creek peters out, at least on the map. Still, it did not occur to me till now that the Blues tradition spawned a band of cross-dressing Long Island malingerers who then planted the seed of the anti-music movement and that I may have had something remotely to do with it. Shit!

Mescaline

Somehow, likely because I was a known psychonaut, I came into possession of a shoe box full of peyote buttons. For the following month, through recording sessions and gig rehearsals I was delightfully mescalinated. Each morning I would clean three buttons of the nauseating strychnine wart fuzz and shove a crusty scab between my cheek and gum as recommended by snuff enthusiasts. By noon things are getting interesting but I'm still able to get through these prog rock Utopia jams so in goes another button. Nobody notices, eventually me also. I later acquire a baggy full of what looks like powdered clay but is purported to be 'organic' mescaline, which we consume by wrapping a small pile of the stuff in toilet paper and washing it down. One night I lose track of the dosage and find myself flat on my back on the roof of the triplex. I think it was shortly after viewing an art house presentation of the rarely screened Flesh Gordon. And why that particular film should have triggered such an episode is unclear.

Finally I realize that peyote is a religious sacrament as much as a consciousness raising tool. It was not my first ego destroying experience involving chemicals, but it was the first time I felt truly alone. I was not being bombarded with hallucinations. Quite the opposite. Complete nothingness. A balloon without a string. A cloud ever dissolving. Did I touch the face of god? What I?

People are convinced they know themselves, when what they've actually done is bought their image of themselves. But we really know little of ourselves. What we do know is that we'd all stop learning or striving if people would just accept us. That allows us to accept ourselves as we are, not as we would secretly like to be. Then we can justify giving up the struggle to be something more like our ideals, like we hope all of us would be.

Susan

Albert thought I needed someone to help me manage the details of my life and career so he introduced me to Susan Lee. She had very big eyes and a round face that reminded me of a wise owl. One of the first things she advised me to do was buy a house, as apparently I was making so much money producing and doing so little with it that I was going to lose a lot to taxes. I didn't really do much house hunting and didn't need to because Susan found a house in Lake Hill with a smaller structure on the property that would make an ideal studio. She also found me a dentist to overhaul my teeth, a doctor who gave lectures and was younger and very disarming while I was in the chair. He even had me in alone on a Saturday and extracted 4 molars from both sides of my face without me chickening out. As I began to do more touring in various configurations Susan became tour manager, traveling around with a bunch of naive boys in an RV. The job would sometimes entail bullying promoters and house managers into doing what they had agreed to do and while she performed such convincingly and effectively, rarely was it necessary since she often achieved the desired result with little more than a tight sweater and a disarming smile. She became unwaveringly loyal to me, protecting me even from Albert's designs and was for a time de facto manager, keeping me out of trouble and dealing with people I was avoiding. She was... mom.

Though I didn't think about it much, it was still pretty unusual to have a woman in charge of a touring band in the mid 70s. I had never thought that women should be artificially limited, even though female cops were rare and firefighters non-existent. But my sister always did better than I in school so naturally would have had a broader range of opportunities. We always assumed she'd become the successful one. The only thing I could do that she couldn't is become a sperm donor.

The paternalistic view of women holds that the uterus is a bug as opposed to a feature and that all of its attendant parts and humours prevent the owner from being capable of the full range of activities available to those without uteri. And while indeed there are differences in height and in bone and muscle mass, for any particular task, save lifting weights with your testicles, an appropriately scaled female will always outperform an inappropriately scaled male. And there has yet to be a man who can give birth to something the size of a watermelon, and it doesn't matter which hole he tries to eject it from.

House

The day came when I decided I was ready to quit the city and move into the Lake Hill house. The first night I camped in a sleeping bag near the fireplace- there was barely a stick of furniture in the place. I bought myself a pickup truck and began hitting all the antique shops in the area and built up a pretty good collection of Mission Oak furniture and vintage lamps and such, my taste having apparently improved radically since the Nichols Canyon experience. I got another water bed, this time built to fit into a more classic looking bedstead with drawers and shelves and such. I bought a small John Deere tractor with a rototiller and started wearing bib overalls when working in the garden. I had a 13' hard video dish installed that had to be at the opposite end of the property from the house so a long trench was excavated for the cables. I had a pond dug behind the house which was fed by siphoning from the creek nearby and about 150' up the mountain. I had a toolshed built and renovated the odd room on the side of the house into a library with vaulted ceilings and where I set up a video projector. This would be the only room warm enough to spend the winter in. I planted blueberries (did poorly) and raspberries (grew like weeds) and a couple of weird hybrid fruit trees which mostly died. I began to learn how to cook. I could play music as loud as I wanted any time of day. I could run around the property naked, weather permitting, since practically nobody knew where the house was. Suddenly, I was Theroux.

The move to Lake Hill exposed me to prolonged aloneness, which turned out to be something I enjoyed. I had the time and space to work on myself and as long as I was doing that I could tolerate being stuck with myself. If 'hell is other people' then perhaps heaven is no other people. Or it may be that I'm the kind of person ideally suited to jail time but I hope never to have to confirm that theory.

It may be that the rarest commodity in the world will soon be solitude. Not the sad kind where you feel like you've been abandoned, but the therapeutic kind where you get away from all distractions so you can hear yourself think. Vast populations already feel naked and vulnerable without a communications device, so if you can't live without a cell phone, it's probably too late anyway. Your innermost thoughts will remain hidden from you.

I was absorbing a lot of new ideas and the conclusion I arrived at was to be more mindful of the everyday choices I made and my willingness to own them, so I decided to give vegetarianism a try. I don't remember the exact moment but I pretty much went cold tofurkey one day and for the next 8 years had no flesh of any kind. Indeed, I got to that very annoying point of asking "Is there chicken broth in that?" every time I ordered anything. Worse, I would sneer at other people's food which made me an awful dinner companion. Touring was a nutritional nightmare because most towns in the 70s never came close to meatless unless there was an Indian restaurant, resulting in a diet that would sometimes be about 50% cheese sandwiches. England was something of a veggie oasis, what with actual chains of vegan restaurants and an Indian eatery on every corner, and notwithstanding the fact that most popular English food was bland and greasy and considered some of the world's worst cuisine. I also got into fasting for a while, not out of any overt spiritual benefit but just to see if I could do it… I think I got up to 10 days once on nothing but cranapple juice. When I finally went back to being omnivorous, wouldn't you know that it was not a fine cut of beef or a broiled chicken, but a hot dog- the best hot dog I ever ate.

The early 70s was, of course, the Vietnam Era. Although the lottery system gave me a very high number which made it unlikely I'd be drafted, I knew that other young men my age were killing and being killed. I was pretty sure I couldn't kill someone, maybe not even in self-defense. Knowing that, what would I be willing to kill? Could I slaughter a pig or a cow while there were still alternatives that didn't require slaughtering, like say, a soybean? How far down the food chain would I go before the pangs are so acute and the revulsion so numb that I am eating insects. Pretty sure I'd be comfortable milking that cow before then.

Unless you are brought up by culture or religion to revere the food you eat, you probably rarely think about it, which I guess is just carelessness. But then again, becoming possessed with what you eat can sometimes diminish the importance of other disciplines- controlling anger, developing mindfulness of where you are and what your options may be, facing the truth about yourself. What you eat doesn't automatically make you a good person, just a less hungry one. However, thankfulness for the meal is always appropriate.

Cameron

My success as a wunderkind and the antics that surrounded it caught the attention of the rock press. Utopia was out on tour when I was informed that a journalist would be following us around for a few dates and I was somewhat amused that he turned out to be a baby-faced teenager named Cameron Crowe on his first major assignment. We were supposed to play a gig in Albuquerque which was canceled for some reason so we opted to spend the off time in Santa Fe. Someone had laid a load of mushrooms on us so pretty much the entire entourage got lit and decided we should go out to the Puye Reservation and watch sunset from the pueblos, duly witnessed the entire time by our dead sober little brother. It did not stop there, as many of us opted for a second dose and after spending the night staring at TV static decided to drive to Taos, a destination we failed to arrive at since we got distracted by a hot spring on the way. We got back to the hotel just after our second sundown whereat Kevin Ellman excitedly hustled us into his room so he could demonstrate the powerful reverb created when he chanted his Nam Myoho Renge Kyo at an incomprehensible sputter. The last thing I remember was the sound of Ralph Shuckett playing a piano somewhere in the echoey hallways and ruing the fact that we had run out of mushrooms.

I'm not sure what Cameron knew about Utopia when he got the assignment to cover us on the road. We weren't famous for our offstage antics but I'm pretty sure I had a psychedelic reputation by then so I guess we must have lived up to that expectation. Actually, I don't recall an episode since wherein the entire band and crew got so... wait, that did happen again! All I remember is an RV, a farm access road, a bunch of fireworks and a trip to the local hospital to get a tetanus shot after catching my Achilles on a piece of rusty barbed wire. And no journalist to witness it.

Young Cameron Crowe, as everyone knows, went on to become a successful writer and film director. His breakthrough was a movie that had nothing to do with rock bands, but rather represented a simple suburban tableaux that a young music journalist never would have experienced since he was instead out somewhere in the New Mexico desert watching a bunch of prog rockers tweak their brains out instead of playing... which would turn out to be a different movie.

World

A lot of what fueled my consciousness expansion was the discovery of a small network of occult bookstores. A little bit of research revealed that in almost any major market I played there would be a local purveyor of Theosophical volumes and Manly Palmer Hall rarities. Some were from the turn of the century when missionaries spread like locusts throughout the Middle East and Asia and the public at large was interested in mystics and magicians like Gurdjieff and Madam Blavatsky. I decided I should follow up on my incessant book collecting and actually go out and experience what I had been reading about so I bought a Pan Am around-the-world ticket. You could make as many stops as you wanted as long as you flew in the same direction. I had a short list of destinations, some of which required visas and others, inoculations. I bought myself a bomber jacket with a hundred pockets and a backpack that I filled with essentials like a first aid kit and maps and a Swiss Army knife (you could fly with one in those days) and one book- Magister Ludi by Hermann Hesse because I had already read Siddhartha twice. The Vietnam War was ended and for the most part the world was not a particularly dangerous place for a hippie with a backpack. I would be following the footsteps of others who were variously looking for spiritual enlightenment or hashish or both. I would be better prepared than most such wanderers as I possessed an American Express card and a couple thousand dollars in traveller's checks.

Since I'd never been to college, I'd never been on sabbatical, that mystical journey of self-discovery that takes you to a far off land and alien cultures. Now I am Candide, a fortunate naif abroad or more likely Siddhartha, anxious to get a snoot full of anything and everything, the whole gamut. If there was a guru out there for me, I was going to find him. If I was destined to find enlightenment at the cost of sanity, I was prepared for that gamble. The most frightening prospect was that I would find nothing of substance at all, only myths and rumors.

For most the world is myths and rumors, unproven facts and untested assumptions. The value of money is the collective faith that everyone has in it. Love is the belief that others really love you, something you hope never to have to prove. Religions demand we believe in personalities we have never met in human form. We cannot see the air that we breathe. To question all these things is an assault on one's own personality, that network of assumptions that informs how you see yourself in the world. Rejection of apparent reality is not for the faint-hearted.

Istanbul

I finally touched down in Istanbul sometime around noon after a re-deye-and-a-half of flying. I had no luggage to collect, only my pack which apparently piqued no interest during customs and I soon found myself in the corridor leading to the street. Before I could think about my next move I was swooped down upon by a clean-cut Turkish youth of about 21 who peppered me with the typical barrage of queries as to how he could be of some monetary value to me. Since I had no plan except to be open to the situation I'd put myself in, I let him shepherd me into a cab and off towards town without any specific agenda. He rattled off myriad possibilities a typical hippie tourist would want to experience (Blue Mosque, hash bar, etc) and eventually asked me if I knew of another American he had 'helped' who had a specific yen to meet some Sufis. I didn't recognize the name, but I did indicate that I was interested in anything unique to the region, Sufis included, and he then went into a whole other gear and jabbered off new directions to the cab driver, lurching us tangentially into a more suburban part of the city. It turns out he is the eldest son of the diplomatic representative of the Istanbul International Airport and is no mere hustler, but about as connected a mensch as I could ever expect to run into. He takes me to his house where I meet his mother, grandmother, siblings and eventually his father. Everyone changes into pajamas as soon as they are home and since they have a guest (me) they bring out a snack of fruit, cheese and honey. Late in the afternoon Hussein decides it is time for us to go to the bus station.

I have always depended on the kindness of strangers. I must confess to a dopey faith in the power of sincere guilelessness, an admission that you really don't have any idea what exactly to do and some 'samaritan' (in the loosest sense of the word) will fill in your blanks. Yet, there must be a line somewhere when the return diminishes compared to the ante. James Bond always seemed to know the precise location of the line. Would love to have seen him played for a sucker when he was, say, only 07 and didn't know the line from his boner to get a license to kill.

Knowledge has a cost/benefit aspect that's hard to calculate, so most people aren't interested in learning experiences that don't look like an outright bargain. The problem is, you don't know what you don't know until after you know it. Meaning what you know is not necessarily what you set out to know. Sometimes you just have to plunge into the unknown to find out anything.

Konya

After an endless bus ride on rutted roads over mountains that brought the temperature down thirty degrees we were finally dropped off at dawn at an intersection in the middle of a vast plain that seemed to have no sign of human life but for the roads. By some miracle a car appears in the distance and soon we are motoring into downtown Konya. By the time we got settled in the 'best' hotel in the city it was afternoon so we spent the rest of the day hitting the tourist spots, which was pretty much the Blue Mosque and the surrounding souvenir shops. The patron saint of the town is Mevlana, also known as Rumi, a very Jesus-like Islamic holy man who preached love and tolerance and the Dervish dance. Hussein tells me that the founding of modern Turkey by Kamal Ataturk entailed the outlawing of the expressions of the various warring Muslim sects and declaring the country a secular state. Thus the Dervishes that tourists would enjoy are not actually the real Dervishes and they are very wary of being caught truly expressing themselves. Nevertheless, the next day he manages to track down the keeper of the Flame of Mevlana who agrees to see me. He is a wizened, slight old man in his late 80s, very friendly and quiet and prefers to be called 'hodja'. We meet in a small sitting room in his house where he resides on a low couch and everyone else on the floor. He seems to slip in and out of consciousness but explains that he is not sleeping, he is communing with Mevlana. Not being much up on Sufis, I have fewer questions for him than he for me, I presume because he has met other seekers from the west looking for 'answers'. He seems to see something worthy in me and says I should come back the next day and he will bestow some insight on me. On the following day he has had no second thoughts about me and presses me to return to Konya on the full moon in May and he will show me how to dance.

As far as I can tell, the idleness of my curiosity may have been what got me in the door with the Sufis. Maybe since they had to maintain such a low profile they were turned off by zealots. I did try to carry myself with some sense of reverence for their tradition, while my guide Hussein would behave like an Islamic class clown and was being constantly berated and cuffed in the head. I'm the only one who doesn't speak Turkish, so just hope they don't get so pissed at him that I'm without an interpreter.

The one true religion is always the one you are born into. The propositions that most religions require you to believe are often so preposterous that they must be forced on you from childhood. To believe something else, to change religions is to voluntarily subject yourself to the same torture, except this time you are not innocent and gullible. This time you know it's preposterous.

Adana

Hussein had a lot more in mind for me, or perhaps was using me to get a free tour of Turkey, but I did get to experience a more indigenous range of exotic adventures as a result. We traveled on to Adana on the southern coast and engaged in activities that a resident might enjoy. I was taken to a barber shop and served sweet black tea from a swinging tray moments before a straight razor was held against my throat, resulting in every sense the closest shave I have had in my life. A little TV is blaring in the background with coverage of a soccer game, a sport that hadn't even crossed my mind since I endured a season not playing it in Junior High but which is, as testified by the regalia that festoons almost every shopfront, a national fixation far more important than the hippie oddball in the barber's chair. Next stop is the bath house, a maze of white tile that is heated by steam generated in a giant furnace behind one wall. Everyone is burly and swarthy with short hair and a beard. I am skinny and pale and have long hair and no beard. And everybody is naked. That evening we have dinner in the best restaurant Hussein can find because, after all, I am paying. I convince him that it's time for me to get on with my journey and we catch a flight next day from Ankara to Istanbul and then to Iran. For now my Ottoman Fantasy is complete.

I never learned a word of Turkish beyond those I already knew like pajamas and baklava. I rarely had any idea what Hussein was saying to other Turks or if I was being accurately represented. I had to put complete faith in someone who I'd met just days before and who had at times raved macho horror stories about killing or at least threatening to kill people for such crimes as looking at his sister the wrong way.

A translator and an interpreter are not at all the same thing. A translator is not supposed to be concerned with meaning, only that the result is literal- nouns and verbs in the right place, tense and person are consistent, pronunciation and inflection are proper. That doesn't ensure that the speaker's intended message was conveyed. That's the job of an interpreter, to convey the intent, the meaning, even if the words have to be changed.

Teheran

As my taxi pulls up to the hotel the first thing I see is a guy heaving a paving stone through another guy's windshield. I'm met at the curb by a very cordial young Tehrani who speaks perfect English and guides me through check in. He offers to make his free time the next day available to me and he seems like a godsend or in this case Allahsend. We meet in the lobby the next morning and he guides me first to the Casbah. It is a small city unto itself, noisy and dusty and chockablock with storefronts of all kinds, especially vending rugs and other Persian specialties. We got to a place where the walkway split and in front of the shop that bifurcated the street was a huge aproned merchant wailing the daylights out of an urchin of about 7 that he had trapped by the collar. Nobody took any notice of this, indicating it was a common sight and likely the way young thieves were discouraged. My guide understands that I am not there to shop and ushers me into the galleries and hovels that are behind the façade where the actual goods are made. Inside a tiny stall is a rug maker. I'm told that his lifetime output will be about a dozen rugs because he will go blind from the wool dust by his early thirties, whereupon he would have presumably passed the time honored tradition down to his soon to be blind children. On our way to our next destination I saw a guy go out of his way to kick a stray dog. We later arrive at a zurkhaneh, a fancy, domed wrestling arena that appeared to be made of white marble. Beefy Persian men displayed their strength and wrestled while teenagers cooed from their pews. At one point a small hubbub broke out and a gentleman was ushered with much pomp to a special seat. As things returned to normal, my guide offered that it was the ambassador from Iraq. I spent that evening in the hotel club where the young and rich discoed to local and international hits. How was I or any of the Persian hipsters in the club to know that a year later the Shah would fall and Americans and Iranians would become such bitter enemies?

I got the impression that Iran and the US were the closest of allies: young men on the street would stop and chat just to practice their English on me. No one every mentioned the Shah's dreaded secret police, presumably trained by the CIA. When the revolution happened I was stunned at the apparent hatred that the Iranians had for us- we seemed like such good friends a year ago. Grudges are for highschoolers. Smart people settle and move on.

The actual Casbah is more than the original shopping mall. It is the template upon which the internet was modeled. The archetypal battle, the incessant conflict of our species is between the guller and the gullible. What can one get away with, both as a provider and consumer, before the jig is up? Come away wiz me to zee casbahhh...

Kabul

The flight from Tehran to Kabul wasn't particularly arduous once the plane got in the air. The 3 am departure brought us over the airfield by 8 and the rising sun cast long shadows from the antediluvian mud huts that crowded the landing strip. Customs was more or less invisible so I hied easily to the Intercontinental Hotel that straddled a saddle-shaped peak between the new and old cities. I had made the assumption that the old city was actually Kabul, so I wended my way down to get a snootful of it. This was as primitive as any place I had ever been and the populace, used to the sight of hash seeking hippies, wasn't particularly fazed by me. I found nothing I would consider buying, no place I would consider eating in, and no vehicle I would consider riding in, so I hiked back to the hotel on the hill and did all my shopping in the concession that seemed designed just for me where I bought exotic instruments and black powder muskets crudely inlaid with mother-of-pearl and which probably would have blown your face off if you tried to fire them. All of it was packed into a galvanized crate that would appear in Lake Hill long after I forgot I sent it. That's all I remember.

My Kabul experience was filled with viscerally intense episodes that seemed natural in context and bizarre in retrospect. I walked through the old town where a wrinkled and antic shade insisted on shaking my hand, and the memory I have is of clasping a foot. I watched a Pilipino cover band in the 'skyview lounge' play dead ringer favorites for an international crowd that was definitely not there for the music while I drank coffee so strong I had to pace the entire hotel 5 times in the wee hours before I could face the walls of my room.

About a year after my one and only visit to Afghanistan the Russians got fed up with the Western listening stations and invaded the country. The futility of that exercise is history. All I know is this: If there's a more primitive place on earth (and there probably is), I haven't been to it. People keep invading the country with the expectation that 'modernity' just hasn't had an opportunity to thrive. Vain bullshit. There will always be places where the past is the only currency.

Delhi

Flying out of Kabul is as much a crapshoot as flying in but I finally touch down in India. New Dehli looks to be a green city, no skyline but a vast forest dotted with a few tall buildings, five-star hotels like the one I'm staying in. Jitney, an open-air motortricycle is the preferred means of travel so I hop one to the old city and the most congested street in town, Chandni Chowk. This is the main shopping district and it's a riotous assault on the senses. The first thing I notice is the symphony of smells: food, chemicals, people, feces, an every-changing combination of powerful odors. The noise has a shrillness to it, echoing the high-pitched chattering that often embodies speech in India. There is no such thing as 'pastel' here, colors are all neon bright primaries and secondaries. Nearby is the Red Fort, a sprawling sandstone artifact of the Mughal dynasty that houses gardens and museums and a particularly opulent style of ornamentation that evokes the glory of an old and exotic empire. In the following days I would explore the capitol in digestible chunks, visiting the gargantuan parliament complex where I saw an ash-covered ascetic running naked around the perimeter of the main building in some act of purification and to no ones apparent interest, or wandering residential neighborhoods, or haunting tourist traps for souvenirs. When it was time to move on to Nepal I had to physically appear at the packed airline office, which took at least half a day. They had none of the high-speed communications that most other countries enjoyed so the process involved a lot of paperwork, telexes and phone calls. When I finally get the flimsy piece of paper that is my 'ticket', I'm not fully confident that I will actually be on that plane.

India is probably the country I'm most interested in experiencing but except for the chaos of Old Delhi, I don't quite feel like I'm getting it. New Delhi is, well, new. It's international, modern by Indian terms and still haunted by British culture-everyone drinks gin and tonic in the hotel bar. While I didn't have a conversation with someone at the other end of the caste system, I sensed that there was still some pride of empire in those who remembered The Raj. "My" India was still out there somewhere.

The British did a lot of damage to the collection of kingdoms that would become post-Raj India, but probably the worst thing they left behind was Indian-style bureaucracy. If the British required two copies of everything, well dammit, we Indians can do better than that- five copies! Of course no one needs to be tutored in abuse of power- anyone who has spent an afternoon at the DMV knows that. Unfortunately, the Indian version of bureaucracy does not have the fastidiousness of the original so the paperwork usually gets screwed up anyway.

Kathmandu

Since I had so few expectations of Nepal's capital, I was commensurately impressed with how much it met my spiritual fantasies. You could not walk more than a few paces before encountering a shrine of some kind, however large or tiny. Every aspect of life was on display in the maze of the old city. One moment a wedding procession completely occupies the width of an alley-sized street, the next a couple of bearers run by carrying a dead body wrapped in a sheet and hung from a bamboo pole like freshly killed game. There is a serenity in the populace, easy smiles everywhere and an efficient but unhurried pace. A half hour bike ride out of town and I am at the site of the largest conclave of Tibetan expats in the world, Bodenath Stupa, a holy dome around which dozens of monasteries have sprung up, the largest of which sits on a hill overlooking the stupa. It is my luck that a public ritual is just starting and I find myself cross-legged on the floor of the great hall with a few hundred other mostly Tibetans, sharing what seems like health mix passed around and listening to the chanting of the lamas. The decor is dizzying, brightly painted dragons and demons, but all the natives seem used to it. Kids are playing and nobody gets particularly 'holy ghosted'- it's almost like a sacred picnic. I pedal back to town feeling that I had justified my journey to the edge of the world.

The second or third night in Kathmandu I awoke in my hostel room with a song in my head that I felt desperate to remember. I had no guitar with me and of course, no ability to think in conventional music notation, so I spent about a half hour visualizing a piano keyboard and how my hands should look to articulate the chords in my head. For the rest of my trip I replayed that exercise until many weeks later when I actually got in front of a piano and made my hands repeat what I had imagined.

To have a musical idea spring so particularly formed into your mind as if to have written itself could be attributed to almost anything or nothing. But you may find yourself in a place and that place speaks to you, coaxes out of you something unexpectedly honest and guileless. Your defenses become impotent before a culture that spans millenia. There is music in everything and you just forgot to notice.

Patna

I returned to India through a relatively quaint town called Patna, relatively meaning not an anthill of people. The Ganges ran through it so I went down to the riverside thinking I might bathe in it. Not gonna happen. For such a holy waterway there seemed to be little concern for how much crap got dumped into it, and I mean literally crap. Bathing next to a turd was more local than I was prepared for so I explored elsewhere. I dared for the first time to try some street food, having been lucky enough so far to have contracted no gut-destroying bacteria. A vendor served me a leaf full of raw peas and onions sprinkled with hot pepper and it was the best thing I had thus far eaten in India. Aside from the river there are not a lot of landmarks I'm interested in so I begin to plan my next move, which is to head off blindly across West Bengal toward Bodh Gaia. I spent most of my second day in Patna trying to negotiate my traveler's checks into enough cash at the local bank to buy a finely crafted Indian motorbike. Once I finally had it in hand, I wasted no time taking possession of the vehicle and promptly dumped it in the gravel median outside the dealership, skinning my elbow in the process. I quickly got control of the pitifully underpowered scooter and headed off into the countryside to go find the site of Buddha's enlightenment.

Up until I left Patna I had pretty much been on the network: I would stay at the nicest hotel I could find, not wanting to risk disease or food poisoning. I had travelled by air everywhere. Now I was about to go off the grid, no hotel reservations, no escort or interpreter, just a map. I probably should have felt more trepidation but once I got on the bike I felt oddly free. I must have had an unreasonable confidence that I would be able to find fuel, under some false assumption that it would be be like rural America.

A full life is a balance of prudence and foolishness. You are never going to discover anything about the world or yourself through constant conservative prudence. Conversely, endless tomfoolery not only tries your friends' patience but can tempt disaster with no reward. Choose carefully your flights of fancy and live to enjoy the memory of them.

Gaia

Rural India is a part of the country I haven't experienced, and it seemingly had not experienced anything like me. If I should pull the bike over at a village for, say, a couple oranges, the entire town turns out to gawk at the long-haired freak in the bomber jacket, and since I speak no local language and no one seems to speak British I become self-conscious and quickly lam out of the village. The countryside is verdant and sweltering, at times offering miles of empty black top without a soul in sight in this most densely populated part of the world. At sunset a thick and blinding swarm of insects rises from the fields along the road, splatting against my face and making it death-defying to try to pass the bus that has more riders on the roof and sides than are inside and which has a perilous center of gravity. My pace slows since I have to remove my shades in the gloaming and I don't want to take a hit directly in the eye. I am relieved to eventually arrive at a town called Gaia with a hotel, that being a stack of whitewashed cubicles, the deluxe suite having a private shithole in the room. Every corner of every hallway is stained red where betel nut eaters have spit their crimson drool. The neighborhood generates a constant din of diesel engines and yelling pretty much 24 hours. I chain my bike up on the ground floor then hunkered on the collapsed mattress reading Magister Ludi by a single stark bulb while lizards festoon the ceiling until I fall unconscious.

In Gaia I saw the face of a dead body for the first time, lying in the train station covered in flies. I was struck with how no one seemed perturbed by this. I was smitten with how, in this milieu, I didn't seem to be as much perturbed as fascinated with how the living casually swarmed around the dead. Maybe this is the custom and maybe I could be customary by acclimating to the obvious... death.

Technically we all die alone in that our death is ours alone. Even if you were to perish in a plane crash or atomic blast, the exact moment of your passing would be unique. That's different from being alone when death comes, to have no one notice or care. To be a statistic but leave no impression. That is the death we dread.

Calcutta

I awoke to find that someone had drained all the gas from my scooter, which can be a problem in a diesel-fueled country. I wheeled around Gaia until I found an oasis of gasoline, then headed off to what I thought would be the shrine of Gaia. Once out on the road I become so frantic to get out of town that I completely overshoot my destination (which is, ironically or appropriately, unmarked) and find myself on the two-lane road that runs through West Bengal to Calcutta. The route is littered with toppled, overloaded semis and bodes the possibility that tigers may jump out of the bush and eat me. About 120 miles outside my destination, and literally in the middle of nowhere, my rear tire goes flat. The REAR freaking tire. I start walking the bike down the road, and lo and behold over the next rise is a repair shop. The mechanic tears into my bike without hesitation. The chain, gears and other small parts are sitting in the dirt while he patches the inner tube, and by some miracle he reassembles everything and I'm on my way. About 20 miles later I give up, hire a cab, throw the bike in the trunk and motor the rest of the way to Calcutta, through nightmarish towns belching industrial pollution. I check into the most spectacular hotel in the city, built during the Raj to the most opulent standards, and spend an hour in a marble lined shower the size of a garage. I spend much of the next day trying to find a way to ship my moped home, but as with everything else in India the seemingly simple becomes impossible. After another day in what is just another big city, I abandon the bike and move on. I fly to Madras in hopes of finding some connection to the original Theosophical Society. The city is blistering hot, just like the food. People walk in the streets and shit on the sidewalks. I find Theosophical headquarters in Adyar on the outskirts of town. The once thriving hub of spiritual exploration was reduced to something like a museum, although they still published books and pamphlets. Nearby was something much more contemporary: Auroville, an experimental city designed by Sri Aurobindo and being built by his followers. There was some truly crazy hybrid architecture and almost nothing was finished, but everywhere there were worker ants slowly realizing the vision. The Future.

I realize that I am only scratching the surface of the vast and variegated mystery that is India. I am fascinated and exhausted less than two weeks after returning from Nepal and not sure my brain can absorb much more. Likely it was foolish to think I could find some spiritual needle in such a gigantic haystack.

Things look so much simpler from a distance. Then you approach and more and more details are revealed until all perspective can get lost. You get hypnotized by it and it takes you over, imposing its vision on you until your first impression is obliterated. Then you surrender… or flee.

Vibhuti

Bangalore was only on my itinerary because I was encouraged by a friend/devotee of Sathya Sai Baba to go check out this supposed miracle man. I hired a car, since it is foolhardy to try to drive a rental in India considering the likelyhood that the car will break down before you run into a cow, stopping first at Puthaparti, the man's hometown. Not there. A young devotee tells me I can and should strive to hook up at an event a day later at his boys school, which I strive to do. The road to the compound is lined with beggars brandishing all manner of disfigurements and infections while the surrounding wall is crowned with broken glass. Once inside I'm struck by the fact that all the westerners are wearing traditional Indian garb while the Indians are all dressed like western businesspeople. Sai Baba is supposed to appear around 11am after about an hour of the crowd singing to coax him out, which is apparently not convincing enough because they must continue for another ninety minutes before his whateverness deigns to make an entrance. There has been a pathway of flower petals prestrewn for him to stride on and everywhere his foot touches acolytes battle to gobble the remains. He blissfully traces the perimeter of the crowd, accepting envelopes stuffed with money and requests for audiences and blessings. Occasionally he produces a puff of vibhuti from his sleeve, a sacred ash I guess you're supposed to rub on yourself. He continues this for over an hour, the attendees singing all the time, then takes a seat on a throne in the center of the compound where he bobs his head in amusement for another twenty minutes then leaves as disciples line up to see if their bribes will be accepted.

I was a bit disappointed that Sai Baba hadn't performed one of his more infamous miracles like puking up stones or materializing designer watches. The production of ash out of a long-sleeved garment did not seem that hard a trick to master. But plainly this was a transactional event- give me the envelope and maybe you'll get more than an eyeful of ash. I was not buying in.

Adoration. Who wouldn't want it? Once you have experienced it, what would you do to keep it? What's any different from being a pop star where people love you because you entertain them, something they find mystifying. Worship is a form of entertainment, all the more so if the object can do magical things like vomit lingams and produce fine timepieces out of thin air… or play the guitar.

Bali

I'm not exactly sure why I went to Bali, which was so far out of my general flight path, but since this was my personal road movie, to Bali I did go. Not having learned my lesson in India, I rented a scooter and took on being my own tour guide with, of course, the usual dumping of the bike in an intersection soon after hopping on. I decided to visit the famous Monkey Temple (there are lots of them throughout the Hindu and Buddhist world) up in the mountains. The first thing you see before entering the grounds is a sign in bold red lettering warning menstruating women not to cross the threshold lest the monkeys go insane. Since it's not my time of the month I boldly motor up the hill and am soon surrounded by trees full of monkeys who are plainly unconcerned and go about their daily lives which seem to consist of a whole lot of monkey sex in every possible configuration including the enviable male behavior of self-felating. When later I was walking on the beach along the luxury strip of hotels the sexily clad tourists seemed so boring by comparison that I left the next day.

I have a running argument with Danny O'Connor that is based, at least between him and me, on a pure hypothetical: if you could blow yourself, would you? I maintain that definitely anyone who could probably should and do so guiltlessly. He is disgusted by the entire concept, as if it was someone else's dick in your mouth. By such logic, masturbation would be equivalent to jerking someone else off. Regardless, who knows better what you like than yourself? Best case scenario you're only going to get the very tip anyway.

I've never understood going to a far off place to do the same things you could do at home. The more a place accommodates the branded expectations of the typical tourist, the less it is that place. Why go to so much trouble to see and smell and do the same thing you could do an hour from your house (depending on the weather)? What kind of adventure is piling into a bus with a bunch of day trippers to take pictures from the comfort of the air conditioning?

Poison

By the time I got to Tokyo I was feeling my trip was coming to a conclusion. The city is modern and much of the populace speaks English and everything is so civilized that I overlook a lot of the finer points of the culture and leave after a few days. I made a perfunctory stop in Honolulu, not really having the energy to visit Kauai before finally making landfall in San Francisco. I've got a couple hours before my redeye to New York so I give Bruce McCaulley a ring and we meet up at a North Beach pizza stand. I'm still vegetarian so I stick with a plain slice of pie. A few hours later I'm getting on the plane and not feeling especially well. About halfway into the blessedly empty flight and I am spewing out both ends with no relief in sight. Suddenly I am experiencing the kind of mental and physical trials that I had expected from the journey now far behind me. I am hallucinating and praying for my life while trapped in a cylinder flying through the air at a fantastic altitude. If there was horrifying turbulence, I don't remember it just as I don't remember how I finally got home and into my sick bed.

How can this be that I have traveled literally around the world and never got sick until I'm almost home? I suppose I should have been grateful that I was on a substantially empty plane and that the attendants spoke English. Still, I had been to some of the filthiest places on earth where there were surely no inspection regimes. Was this to be the ultimate takeaway, delivered via food-borne bacteria?

Phileas Fogg ballooned around the world in 80 days on a wager with no other object than to win the bet. According to the popular film version he was accompanied by a manservant and acquired a girl along the way and never got sick from the food. He also seemed to have little respect or appreciation of any of the cultures he encountered on the way, probably because most stops were at outposts of the British Empire. In the end he nearly loses because his precious watch, the thing that has paced him through this race, is off by an hour. Victory. Never smelt the roses... or the vomit.

Dervish

I returned as instructed to Konya during the full moon in May, often referred to as the Wesak Moon by Wicans which is probably not a coincidence. Hodja instructs me in the basics of Muslim life, the first hurdle being the ablutions which involve inhaling water up your nose and since it feels a little like drowning takes some getting used to. Everything else seems easy by comparison until it comes to the spinning lesson. One hand is held to Allah, the other to the earth and with a little bit of footwork you might be able to keep it up for thirty seconds before you succumb to vertigo. On the final night of the week Hodja's closest adherents assemble in the tiny apartment and the shit gets serious. Hodja explains why I am there and why they should stop glaring at me and get on with the spinning. A couple older guys do a little brief symbolic rotations then a pretty large guy gets up and commands the small rug in the center of the room. He turns slowly and gracefully at first, establishing a tempo for the accompanying 'hu hu hu' by the seated dervishes. He begins to pick up the pace and twenty minutes later he is a blur as we all hyperventilate but this is not the climax. He spins ever faster as everyone grows dizzier until some unseen threshold is crossed and the entire room slows down like a car out of gas. The next day I broached the possibility of bringing Hodja to the US so he could demonstrate the ritual for the rest of the band, like they would be interested. This set off a whole brouhaha amongst his followers arguing whether he should go and if so who should accompany him. Then came the flood of requests from the entire neighborhood to provide vacuum cleaners and American jeans and Parker pen and pencil sets. When I returned home I tried to make arrangements for him but the language gap and bureaucratic hurdles essentially doomed the idea and that was the last contact I had with the Dervishes.

Though it didn't occur to me at the time, getting dizzy was probably my and most people's first out of body experience. Twirl around until you lose control and laugh hysterically just as if you were drunk. There are probably a few other ways to get high instantly without drugs like pressing your eyeballs really hard, but at some point, maybe around autoerotic asphyxiation, you should draw the line.

The mind is never satisfied with 'reality' nor should it be. And the moment to moment labor of maintaining such reality can be pretty exhausting. There are many paths to respite but few to permanent relief. Who can begrudge someone resorting to the simple and dependable? When the minibar is empty you're going to hyperventilate anyway. May as well enjoy it.

Meatloaf

I'm getting pretty busy as a producer so when Moogy approaches me with the idea of partnering if he can find something I'm interested in I decide to take him up on it. A few weeks later he says he has a candidate named Meat Loaf, a name familiar to me only from having seen The Rocky Horror Show on Broadway. We arrange to have a live audition, which is kind of unusual since most acts would have a demo tape, but apparently this is how they want me to experience it. Aside from the Big Man, in attendance were Rory Dodd and Ellen Foley singing backgrounds and 'evil' mastermind Jim Steinman at the piano. They performed most of what would become Bat Out Of Hell with all the trademarks that would characterize the act- the surprisingly limber giant stalking around mopping his brow, the glowering phantom at the keys, the spectacle of a tiny girl clinging to the hip of a behemoth. At the conclusion of the presentation they talk about how every other producer that has seen what I have just seen has turned them down and I can understand why. Nothing about this would seem to make commercial sense. And that is one reason why I decide to take on the project. We assemble a band that is half Utopia, half E Street Band and begin rehearsal at Turtle Creek with the intention of recording the album as live as possible. About a week in Meat and Steimy express that they would like Moogy off the project. Then the day before we are to start recording Meat tells me his label doesn't understand him and he wants off it. I manage to get Bearsville to fund the record with a right of first refusal, probably not realizing that a symphony orchestra would eventually be involved as well as a substantial payment to a former sportscaster. In the end Bearsville did refuse the record, as did many other labels for months. It looked like I was going to lose a very expensive gamble.

Everyone saw the same act that I saw, but then nobody saw it the way I saw. In my mind this was the genius spoof of Bruce Springsteen that the world so desperately needed. The hyperbolic lyrics about motorcycles and switchblades, the simple triads of the music, the melodrama, the mysterious Svengali at the piano, all fronted not by a hunky denim clad stud but a 250 pound wild man whose head might explode any second. I was sold.

Motive. If you were on trial for murder, your justification would determine your sentence. No one saw commercial success in Meat Loaf's future, but that was not my motive. I wanted to make a statement about the whimsy of pop music and for some reason, that translated into almost obscene success. If that had not occurred to me I might have turned the project down and this page would not exist.

John Siegler was the last original Utopian to retire so we had to audition bass players. A young kid named Kasim Sulton showed up and while he didn't have John's funk factor, he had a voice so we decided to take him on despite the fact that it meant a move to a more pop direction. The new quartet's first project was a high-concept album and tour based on a neo-Egyptian theme, the centerpiece being a sun-worshipper's anthem, ergo the title RA. The recording process went well enough considering we were all getting used to the new lineup. Since arena-scale productions were what everyone was doing we devised a set that consisted of a 25' tall pyramid of steel pipe painted gold, a 12' high sphinx with a laser coming out its forehead, smoke out its nose and paws that extended to the front of the platform everything sat on, and a drum riser surrounded by a moat with dancing water jets in it. Our big production number featured an earth/wind/fire/water series of metaphorical trials. Roger was fire and would nightly battle a Chinese parade dragon with a laser attached to his portable keyboard while pillars of flame shot up around the stage. Kasim was wind and fought through a gale of stage smoke, occasionally dodging tumbleweeds we would pick up on the highway. Willie was water, in some ways the most dangerous stunt because the jets would make the stage wet, often causing Kas or me to slip and fall, sometimes into the moat itself. My stunt was earth, in which the pyramid itself represented a mountain. We had welded foot plates up the front legs of the pyramid and a winch with a hand strap at the top. Nightly I would scale the mountain, slip my hand into the strap between my legs and do a forward flip, noodling guitar throughout. Anyone who saw that show never forgot it, as I am often reminded.

People often ask "How did you do that? Weren't you petrified?". While my pyramid climb was perilous, once I got my hand in the noose I felt pretty secure, although I had only done the stunt twice in rehearsal. That because our sound man insisted on trying it before I did, left too much slack on the wire connected to the strap, and plummeted right into the drum kit. If I was going to fuck my shit up, I was going to do it in front of an audience.

It is remarkable to see the old Kinescope of the Beatles playing in the round in Washington DC. The small Vox amps on chrome tubing stands, the simple 2-toms/2-cymbals drum setup on a little round foot-high riser. The entire rig would have fit in a panel truck-probably did. Halfway through the brief set the band moved the equipment 180 degrees, no roadies except for a little help turning the drum riser around. A decade later a band isn't a band unless they've got a fleet of semis and tour buses. One thing the Beatles weren't responsible for.

Leslie

Meat Loaf did accomplish something during the disastrous Bad For Good sessions. He got married. He did it at my house. I wasn't present at the formal proposal but I witnessed what might have been the defining moment in the courtship when Meat presented Leslie with about eight pounds of whole smoked salmon he brought from the city and proffered to her as if it was as sincere a token of affection as any more traditional gemstone could every be. It must have worked. Everybody knows I'm not a marriage kind of guy which makes my hosting the event (actually the second at the Woodstock house- Eric & Janis tied the knot there) all the more burlesque. It's the dead of winter and it's a challenge for everyone just to get up the drive. The road crew is wearing swag jackets custom made for the event with the date emblazoned on the back like it was just another tour stop. The Episcopalian minister performing the rite is almost an hour late and he's about 90 years old and in the care of a sincere young assistant. Every word of the ceremony has to be whispered in his ear and he looks at Meat and says "Do you Leslie take Marvin to be your lawful wedded wife" and as far as I'm concerned I have never been forced to attend a more perfect nuptial. For the next few hours the menfolk go out and slide their cars into ditches and other cars and spend a lot of time spouting about how to undo the mess and grunting and sweating in proof or disproof of the various theories. And of course it would be not a few years before Meatloaf would have another hit record.

I've never imagined being married. I've imagined and actually lived a life that some people would say resembles marriage but I've never dreamed, as I've heard women do, of standing in front of a bunch of people and making proclamations about what I intend to do for the rest of my life regarding my sleeping situation. I can't imagine wanting something so badly that I would openly lie to a select group of invitees that would presumably include close friends that I'd hope would continue to respect me.

Is it hypocritical to host the marriage ritual when you have little belief in the outcome? The witnesses are whispering their doubts to each other. The unwed are looking to score something both memorable and forgettable to make the effort of showing up worthwhile. You are affirming a fantasy or enabling a tragedy. Hypocritical? All too typical. Divorce is so easy.

Preggers

Things seem to be going a little better in my world since I managed to get the Lake Hill house to myself. There was a lot of production going on in the 'barn' and I had no emotional encumbrances to speak of. Bebe had been gone for weeks tagging Aerosmith around Europe so that unfortunate episode in my life seemed to have been rested. Then I got the call. Pregnant again she said. Not Steven she said. Timetable says it's me. Please can she come "home" she says. Fuck fuck fuck fuck fuck.

That last part actually belongs in this paragraph. This is crazy this is crazy this is crazy. How do you contest the testimony of a pathological liar? Maybe I really am the sperm donor even though she is quite obviously fucking her way across Europe with a notorious priapus? I should tell her outright that it's not my problem. If it was, get rid of it.. but what if it's his 'problem'? Am I supposed to solve his problem? Fuck fuck fuck fuck fuck.

That last part REALLY belongs in this paragraph. I have planned always to plan my children and to especially plan who to have them with since, you know, you're both having them. But as previously noted, I take childhaving very seriously in that they can't be unhaved and should never be made to feel like an accident. Take that breeders.

Kaiju

I had made a point of not letting Bebe move her possessions into the Lake Hill house. Little by little she snuck things into the closet but mostly obeyed the edict. Our relationship was down to a week or two a month of cohabitation but we were pretty much unlinked and I felt like an amicable extrication might be possible, especially when she began traipsing around with Steven Tyler. Then the 'news' that she was pregnant and the claim of my paternity which I could not scientifically refute, compounded by my pesky concern for the unborn kid, resulting in an unhappy cohabitation and the ruination of my pastoral peace of mind. One Sunday morning I hear her ranting on the phone to someone in that harpy tone and 15 minutes later a car screeches into the drive. The front door flies open and Susan storms in and Bebe flees up the stairs. Susan corners her on the bed and starts whaling on her and vilifying her in no uncertain terms and I realize this has something to do with the phone call and also that I have never before or since seen the usually serene Susan Lee performing an act so uncharacteristic. After a minute of beratement that I somehow felt powerless to intervene she left without explanation as quickly as she arrived. I never found out what the provocation was.

My feelings at seeing Bebe undergo the kind of beatdown I had so often contemplated myself delivering left me with decidedly mixed feelings. Should I feel guilty, knowing how much she must have deserved it? Was I cowardly that I had no hand in it or in stopping it? Am I remorseful that I have forced my friends and associates to deal with a problem I couldn't or wouldn't resolve?

One morning you wake up and realize you've been sleeping with a Kaiju, a Godzilla-like creature that destroys things out of blundering ignorance with no particular goal in mind. Then the Kaiju rolls over and smiles at you and says it loves you and you tell yourself you can tame it. But no matter how many times you tell yourself that lie, still you wind up introducing the Kaiju to even further landscapes to destroy.

Susan Lee was too upset after her altercation with Bebe to continue as tour manager so we needed a quick replacement. Eric Gardner had been in charge of the massive production that was the RA tour and was fortunately available to take over. We hadn't paid a whole lot of attention to him since most of his work was with the crew but he seemed even-tempered and we had no one else in mind so he was suddenly promoted. As time went by he began filling in other responsibilities a band without a manager needed done and eventually we formalized the arrangement. His fastidiousness and patience served him well as we tended to mock everyone's personal quirks once we got used to them. Eric liked to tell puns, the groanier the better, especially if it took a stupid amount of time to get to the punch line. He had a thing about food that was more than simply enjoying it. Ordering a meal with him was like watching someone describing their dream companion to a dating service. Nothing was ever selected right from the menu without the most detailed customization, to the point that he had to be forced to order last so that the rest of the table didn't rebel. He survived the breakup of Utopia after our swansong tour with The Tubes and continued thereafter to handle my affairs despite the fact that he has several times nearly killed us both while phoning and driving.

Because artist/manager relationships can be notoriously fiery and contentious it's unusual to have a decades-long relationship and I have to conclude that in the case of Eric and me, it's because we have no written contract. Our relationship could be dissolved at any moment and that has caused us to be very adaptive, he to my whims and I to his focus on the bottom line.

The average person does not know what a 'personal manager' is and the term itself has dubious currency within the community of personal managers. It is sometimes a way to brag about the intimacy of your relationship with your artists but doesn't imply that those relationships are healthy or that you are especially good at representation. But it must be acknowledged that there have been mystical manager/artist relationships behind phenomena like Elvis Presley and The Beatles. Likely without Brian and The Colonel we'd have never heard of either.

Bean

I was in Dallas for a Utopia show and was so perturbed with my situation, what with Bebe's late term pregnancy and an impending birth that I was dreading, that I had to venture out to what I knew would be be a long way to go on a lane called Bluebird to witness some questionable entertainment. I did my usual sulk in the corner and was stunned when a tall, skinny, not-cowgirl came over to chat me up. She had a big generous smile and blazing red hair and laughed at everything I said and her name was Karen. I was immediately smitten with her, and apparently she with me. She had a car so we went wherever she felt like until we got to my hotel. At one point she took me to a banking plaza and pointed out a coven of witches who worshipped there- turns out it was just an abstract sculpture in the security lighting and evidence of her weird sense of humor. When we finally alit in my room we were naked pretty fast. We enjoyed each enough to develop a long distance romance, occasionally hooking up in Dallas or some other city. She laughed at my jokes and would tell me she missed me. I didn't tell anyone about her lest Bebe find out and devise a new special hell for me. I had no idea how long my bliss might last.

Wow, I'm thinking. How do I resolve the misery of mere hours ago with the sudden presence of this faerie queen from Deep Elum? As if I was the mortal she needed to transformed her into the angel she was meant to be, swooping down and enveloping me in her wings and... her name was Bean.

Finding the ideal mate is not an intellectual exercise and could never be reduced to an online service. Happiness is not nature's objective. Ideal humans are not grown in vats. Signals that don't even reach the conscious senses tell you this is the person you should breed with. You may be in for a world of ecstasy or misery, but this is your fate, for the sake of humankind.

Liv

By the time Bebe was ready to give birth, they had such things as birthing rooms, which are supposed to make the process less hospital-like. As labor progressed, so did her demand for medication. She did not seem at all prepared for this kind of discomfort on behalf of another person. There was a lot of yelling, which not only mooted the point of the birthing room, but made me even more uncomfortable at my first birthing. I once again shuttered my doubts and tried to be useful as if this was the plan all along. Liv was born healthy and beautiful. When we checked out of the hospital, I had to sign the birth certificate. I took Bebe aside and told her I would only sign if she never disputed my paternity. She agreed. I signed. Once again I was a fool to her. We made the drive silently from NYC to Lake Hill, me not knowing what to say and her being for once wise enough not to provoke me.

Suddenly I am at a place which tests all my declarations about the sanctity of childbearing, which Bebe does not seem to take seriously at all. I have sworn to myself that no child of mine will feel unloved, yet I am pretty sure this is no child of mine. I had always thought that this event would be a celebration and a new beginning, but instead it bound me to someone I had vowed never to breed with and worse, was perhaps the most unfit candidate for motherhood I could imagine. I'm in hell.

We make promises to people and are thus expected to attempt to keep them. If we consciously break them we are not to be taken seriously when we promise something. But promising to yourself is another thing. Can you live with not taking yourself seriously, with making excuses to yourself you know are lame because, well, it is you after all? Especially when you are the only one who knows what you have promised yourself. Especially when someone may use that to make a putz out of you.

Enough

The last day Bebe and I spent under the same roof could have been like any other miserable day with Bebe- the typical carping and dissatisfaction because of my continued refusal to feel affection for her instead of betrayal and entrapment, the endless maneuverings and flimsy evidentiary allusions to get me to cop to her lie, the innumerable trips to the studio, ostensibly to work but spent only in depressed rumination. That afternoon I was sitting on the bridge staring into the pond and Bebe brings Liv out and insists that I hold the baby, something I have been in too much turmoil to be comfortable doing yet, especially in front of the ultimate opportunist. So while my arms are occupied she picks a fight over one of her typical gripes and climaxes by slapping me in the face and then grabbing the baby to use as a shield against retaliation. I'm now more furious than depressed and the rest of the day does not go well. Late that evening I go out to call Bean and cry on her shoulder, which she's getting pretty sick of. Bebe rarely comes down to the studio but I have locked the doors anyway, and sure enough there she is pounding and bellowing that blood-curdling banshee screech I've heard echo down the streets of so many of the world's great cities. This time she completely miscalculates the residual rage I'm feeling and I go totally medieval, matching her decibel for decibel, throwing an old dog dish at her and chasing her around with a hammer which I bang on everything in my path to punctuate my incomprehensible screaming. She finally believes I may cause her injury and flees back to the house yelling "You're crazy, you're crazy!", and with that I have no argument. I call Tommy Edmonds and tell him to remove her before I kill her and then stomp off down the road to Willie's house, about 8 miles away. By the time I get there it's way early morning and I break in so as not to wake anyone and fall asleep on the couch. The next day Bebe and Liv are permanently gone.

As contradictory as it sounds, there is a certain calm logic in insanity. I remember thinking "Yes, I must be crazy, this is how a crazy person acts", and that I must continue to act this way as a matter of self-preservation. You want the constantly mounting anxiety to abate and when it doesn't, it mutates. You become calm. Very calm and very crazy. You're acting crazy and thinking "What's wrong with that? How else am I supposed to act?".

I never did hit Bebe with a hammer or any other object, much as she may have deserved it. It is ironic though that I should have spent so many years as her personal Jesus and would exact my liberation so symbolically. Picture Christ getting off the cross and chasing his torturers around with the hammer they used to nail him up. Of course he never would have hit anybody, but churches would have hammers hanging in the altars instead of crosses.

Programming

Utopia was playing in SF and staying at the Hyatt on the Embarcadero, the hotel that played so pivotally in Mel Brooks' High Anxiety. Of course being in any tall building in San Francisco can induce vertigo by picturing it in the throes of a tectonic disruption. The blind side of the building has a pyramidic slope to it that would suggest possible escape routes from imminent franchise collapse if one was acrobatic enough. Anyway, Roger announced he was going to a computer store a couple blocks down California St to get an Apple II Plus because it had enough balls to actually write real programs in a real programming language called Pascal. This seemed to me to be a great income disposal opportunity so I went along, liked the demos, and took Roj's advice and bought what he bought. Over the next year I fell under the thrall of the infernal machine and did pretty much nothing but acquire new software and accessories and spend day and night learning to program. I had seen a digital paintbox running at the New York Institute of Technology and got it into my head to reproduce it on my little Apple. I got far enough along that on one of my trips to the Bay Area I decided to take it down to the single nondescript building in Cupertino that then housed Apple Computer.

It's hard to describe what it's like to write hard core computer code. You are dealing with an idiot savant that can do very simple things very fast- kind of like Rain Man counting toothpicks. But I mean you have to tell it everything in excruciating yet simple minded detail if you want even the slightest expected result, which you rarely get. It understands precisely 127 words that must be delivered in exactly a certain order. It keeps you awake at night pondering what is going on in that tiny brain and why does it never seems to understand your intent?

Computer coding is a particular kind of problem solving. Unlike dealing with humans, there are few gray areas. There may be several ways to solve the problem, but if the end result is unsatisfactory it won't be because the machine didn't do exactly what you told it to do. That's why solving the problem can be so exhilarating. The results are infinitely reproducible. Unlike the 'solutions' to human problems which usually no one is fully satisfied with and are practically impossible to reproduce.

Kelly

I was doing a week or so of gigs at The Roxy in LA for the recording of Back To The Bars and started to become something of a must-see act because of the unexpected guests that would sit in. There were celebs in the audience almost every show, just as there had been in New York for the Bottom Line sessions. At some point a spate of gift-giving broke out and over the course of a couple days I was handed onstage, amongst other extravagant items, a pure-bred puppy and a cockatoo. And every night front and center was a young girl with streaked hair and feathers and a peculiar personal style who beamed and screamed at every number. We made her acquaintance, learned her name was Kelly Tokerud and that she was 16. When we got to the end of the run she told us she was desperate to get out of LA and would very much like to be our housekeeper, so we got her a ticket. Fortunately we had a spare room for her and she set out right away tidying up and running errands and cooking what she knew how to cook. We had no kids yet so she kind of became our teenage daughter, us taking her everywhere we went and getting her a little powder blue Beetle which she drove... well, like a teenager. After a while it became apparent that she should, as children do, move on and start a career so we sent her to design school and years later I would I would be the audience in Oakland when she received her degree in architecture.

When Liv was less than 6 months old Bebe gave up trying to play mom and gave her to her cousin's family to be raised in a normal household in Portland, Maine. I had a gig that was close enough that I rented a car and drove to visit her without Bebe around, just to see how I felt. I was full of anxiety when they brought me the baby and left me alone for an hour with her. I laid on the couch with Liv on my chest and we both fell deep asleep. When I woke up, she was my daughter.

Kids grow up in Southern California faster than almost anywhere else. Some have careers when they are fifteen, others, drug overdoses at 11. This is only to point out that some places are appropriate to certain behaviors. In LA nobody seems to care if you show up at school, or if you suddenly get a whim to follow a musician to the other end of the country. Not all kids are the same, of course, but there is no denying that parenting in Lala Land is a lot more laissez faire than what most of us are used to.

Planets

We made a deal with RCA to create content for the new laser disc format and since I was way into Tomita at the time I thought his synthesized version of Holst's Planets would make an ideal soundtrack for a video, so I took over Studio A at Bearsville and began filling it up with sets and equipment. The success of Bat Out Of Hell and a new, cheaper format in professional recording equipment allowed me to build a serious collection of broadcast quality devices. I was fascinated with the effects that had gone into Star Wars and sought to use similar technology but with electronic media. Jane Millett had come a long way since the second Utopia album cover, graduating from art school and ready for professional work so I hired her to create models and miniature sets and background paintings for a story about a little boy's dream about space travel. I premiered Side A at a convention that was supposed to be about the laser disc but it was already becoming apparent that the format wasn't really taking off and RCA declined to fund the completion, eventually withdrawing their products from the market. Jane went on to become a fine artist and found her own design firm while I accepted an offer from Albert Grossman to rent a building from him to house the video equipment that would be designed to my specs. While we strove for years to make a business out of it, and while we created a lot of fun video we were too far from civilization to compete and eventually got locked out by Albert when we fell behind in the rent. Everything got sold off and I was done with video for a while.

When most people come into money they usually do something sensible like save or invest it, or something stupid like spend it on a boat. I guess plowing all that Meat Loaf money into a video studio could be interpreted either way. If only we had made the rent I might looked like a genius instead of a self-indulgent auteur. The truth is I never seriously evaluated the commercial possibilities until after I bought all the stuff anyway. I just wanted to make video.

One thing is sure about technology: what is expensive today will soon become affordable, but likely be replaced with something expensive. The challenge has been to get into the game when the market is low and try to compete with tech that is new but rare because of the cost. Happily, as tech becomes smaller and cheaper the gap between the most affordable and the most professional has narrowed to the point that the only parts that can't be made smaller and cheaper are not digital- you're still going to have to pay a small fortune for a good lens.

Wave

A kind of dream came true when Patti Smith asked me to produce her fourth album. I had always wanted to do something creative with her and even though it was a PSG record I was let on to a secret that the band was not supposed to know- that she was going to Michigan to build a family with Fred and this would be the last record for a while. I was somewhat torn how to approach it since I was always biased towards her poetics and she was coming off a radio hit co-written with Springsteen. The presumed single was Frederick, a very uncharacteristic love song that kind of needed an uncharacteristic production in an album of mystical and sometimes angry and militant songs. There was not a lot I could offer as guidance since the inner dynamic of the band, fragile as it was, didn't need outside meddling. Fred never appeared at the sessions, but was everpresent in that he was giving Patti constant feedback throughout the process, which did not bother me but didn't help me understand any better what the target was. Still, I was happy spending time around Patti and helping out as much as I could. The record was released to mixed reviews, which probably didn't bother her that much since soon after she retired from the biz and became a wife and mother.

Something that always attracted and intimidated me about Patti is her intrinsically mystical nature. She always seemed to be channeling something from a place that few people ever got in touch with. Though it never seemed that she was seeking celebrity she was destined to be noticed and it just so happened that 'punk' music was the handiest vehicle. And while the noise drowned out a lot of the subtleties of her performance, the form was all about freedom and Patti has always been about taking advantage of any freedom she had. I envied her.

There is a hierarchy of approaches to engaging an audience. 'Entertainer' is the entry level position, requiring that you simply divert people with whatever it is you're doing- could be something as simple as driving a nail into your skull. Next up is 'performer', someone who can demonstrate a skill that the average person doesn't possess, such as being able to play the most bass drum beats in a minute. Rarest of all is the 'artiste' whose expression cannot be predicted (even by said artiste) and the valuation of such expression is often impossible to categorize. There is no special glory or shame in any of these forms of presentation. You find your comfort level and usually stay there, although if you want to be assured a living, 'performer' is probably the way to go.

Robbery

I'm computing on a typically boring autumn evening in the country when I hear some kind of racket going on at the front door. Yelling and scuffling ensue in the hallway and the next thing I see is some guy in a cheesy ski mask with a gun trying to claw his way around Kelly and into the library. She trips him up, knocking his mask off for a second, and his elbow goes through a pane in the vaulted door, which opens out so he has a hard time getting through it. For some incomprehensible reason, probably because I thought he was a troubled loner, I decide to join the fray and get whacked in the head with a nickel plated roscoe and the guy is screaming at me how stupid I am and even now I must agree with him as I remember peering down the barrel. He is of course not alone and during the course of the next few hours he and three other merry masked adventurers demand to know where the giant drug cache is, threaten to cut off my fingers if I don't divulge the location, hold us at gunpoint for a couple hours as they violently ransack the house while destroying or misplacing anything that was fenceable, try to be clever by singing tuneless renditions of old Nazz songs, tie us up with the only thing they can find (telephone cords. Bean was about 7 months pregnant so they tied her to a chair- me and Kelly were hogtied, she battling and protesting the whole time), toss excess booty onto the lawn when it doesn't fit in the van and pierce the tires on both cars. Due to some pitiful whining at a more sympathetic felon ('My hands are numb, man!'), I got my bonds loosened so I was out about five minutes after they finished and pounding on the neighbors door moments later. Of course, no one was ever charged.

Some experiences put you in a frame of mind unique and potent to the point of incomparability. The first time you have a gun pointed at your head by an unidentifiable entity whose relationship to the trigger is unknown, your first assumption is that this will be your last assumption. That you always wondered what the moment of your death would be like and you are about to find out, and maybe your last thought is to thank God it wasn't in an airliner. It's a high you get a whiff of when you nearly kill yourself on the highway. Then if you don't die immediately you begin to imagine things worse than dying, like you or someone else being kidnapped and mailed back in pieces. Whatever the gun says. The sight of it pulls a trigger of compliance in your mind.

Before this incident, and rarely since, I had not witnessed many acts of physical heroism such as I would have enjoyed had I done the Nam thing. That night I saw little Kelly go hand-to-hand with an armed and drug enhanced malevolence to protect me and my household. That selfless act more than compensated for the pedestrian worthlessness of the intruders.

Rex

Bean started having contractions about mid-morning so we called the doc and made our reservation for the birthing room that afternoon. Having experienced only one other of these procedures and not being a woman I had no expectations about how she would weather the storm and probably neither did she. But however painful the process might have been for her no one in the room had any sense of it, she never complained for a moment. Labor only lasted a few hours after we got to the hospital. Rex was born normal sized with a full head of blond hair. He grew quickly and refused to crawl, pulling himself up on the furniture until he could walk without support, which was at about 6 months. He seemed to never sleep when we slept, if he slept at all, howling into the wee hours until, in a nocturnal rage I hauled his crib to a more distant end of the house, which only made his wailing sound more spooky. Just the three of us up on the mountain in the winter snows... ya get the picture?

Not having grown up with a lot of Old World family traditions I was touched by how important the birth of my first son seemed to everyone around us. And while all the attention was gratifying, it occurred to me that a switch had been flipped. Before Rex was born Bean was getting all the attention... everybody loves a pregnant lady. Suddenly her job was done and I was the proud deliverer of the sperm that got the whole deal started. And after that all I did was watch. It was very Godfatherish.

Nature is constantly yelling at us "Breed, Breed Breed!". It's so easy to get knocked up or knock somebody up that we've had to devise clever methodologies to thwart nature from overbreeding us. Fortunately that gives us the option to remove the sex act from the equation and focus on who might be the best breeding partner and when would be the best time to take advantage of that possibility. Or you could just succumb to nature and bang anything you see and deal with the consequences whenever.

Tornabene

I first met Joel Tornabene at a Utopia show in San Francisco. He and The Tubes were part of the town's inner circle of weirdos so when I signed on to produce what would become Remote Control, Bean and I found ourselves encamped in Joel's guest bedroom at his apartment over the gallery that he ran- Art For Arts Sake on Harrison near the Bay Bridge. While it certainly was a gallery, art wasn't Joel's primary business. There was a closet-sized vault at the back of the ground floor and as if being inducted into some secret society, I was given a tour of its contents. There were some valuable works stashed inside, but their potential worth was entirely overshadowed by the 50 gallon drums full of weed and the stacks and stacks of the true artwork: reams of blotter acid, maybe 500 hits to a sheet, each emblazoned with a little picture of Donald Duck. My life became a daily routine of serious studio work in the day and hedonistic excess every evening, what with constant deliveries of Cristal by the case and oilers as fat as your fuckfinger. Anyone hip who came to town somehow wound up at Joel's. We would occasionally leave the loft to visit other events around town in his giant DeVille convertible which he drove way too fast down Harrison while regaling us in the back seat and hardly ever looking ahead. That pretty much was Joel in a nutshell. Also, he was super gay.

I've never been an extroverted personality but I am perfectly happy to take advantage of someone who is and accrue all the benefits that come with the company of a maniac that somehow trips on the edge of disaster and always lands butter side up. Though I was on occasion horrified at the possible outcomes, I was always surprised at what Joel could get away with. I think it may have been that people were simply stunned.

If we see a stranger breaking the law we call a cop. When we see a friend or relative committing a crime we have a range of options and the police are usually the last resort. You may, ironically, believe it's none of your business. You may even suddenly decide that it's not a crime at all. Why would we make such exceptions? Perhaps because we'd like to be extended the same courtesies should we ourselves wind up on the wrong side of the law.

Suicide

Since I had been such a fan of the band, it was a special treat to produce a record for them. Things are going pretty swimmingly with the Cheap Trick record when the phone rings and it is Mallory at the other end. I haven't seen or heard from her since attending Randy's bizarre out-of-the-blue nuptials to someone none of us had ever met. She quickly cut to the chase- Randy had shot himself. Dead. She adds that he had, unbeknownst to me, been institutionalized and had been talking about suicide and had easily procured a gun which everyone but me was aware of and without further adieu, ended it. Needless to say, the session was over for few days. There is no denying that I was not as engaged as I should have been for the remainder.

What hurts so much when a loved one decides they can't take it anymore is that most of the time they don't give you a chance to say goodbye. Maybe I wouldn't have had so many vivid dreams of Randy, still his old brilliant self, that I had to one by one rebury. Even as I write there is a dissatisfaction, a dangling thread. That after all of our history, I guess I just became a speck on the horizon.

There are things you expect to be there, even if you are never aware of them until someone announces they are gone. You forget that the McRib sandwich is for a limited time only, so you only have one every other day, then once a week. Then you wake up in the night with a strange craving and as you pull up to the clown box you have to face the fact that it's no longer on the menu.

Apple

I had been working on my paintbox program for about a year and on a trip to the Bay Area decided I would drive down to Cupertino and try to find this Apple company. It turned out to be a block long single-story occupancy and it was as easy to walk into as finding the door. Once in, it wasn't long before somebody recognized me- Andy Hertzfeld, a principle engineer was also from Philadelphia and he cheerfully toured me around the building and introduced me to other team members who may have totaled 20 people at the time. I set up my Apple][Plus and demonstrated what I was working on and sometime during that half hour Steve Jobs arrived to catch a glimpse. Steve mentioned that Apple was considering a 3rd party software line called Special Delivery and that since they were going to release their own graphic tablet hardware, this would be an ideal fit. I accepted the paperwork and a prototype Apple tablet and a few months later The Utopia Graphic Tablet System was released. I think I made 10 or 15 thousand dollars, much of which offset the advance I took: a soon to be useless marketing mistake called the Apple III. On a subsequent visit I was NDAed and led to a smaller building where they were working on the next big hardware product. It was called Lisa and it had this weird little interface device called a mouse. You could click on little images called icons that would start applications in boxes called windows that ran programs like text editors and drawing environments. I was amazed because of the radical newness of it even as I was disappointed that it had a black and white screen. They also showed me a much smaller hardware variation called a Macintosh that displayed a little smiley picture of itself when it started up. I wanted one.

As I got to know many of the engineers at Apple I was somewhat amused to discover that almost all of them played an instrument. Of course coders and players would be fascinated and comfortable with the mathematical nature of music. I guess it was more unusual for a successful musician to suddenly commit to learning the alien skill of composing in code, but as the technology penetrated the public consciousness at large it couldn't help but hook in a few players who would succumb to that which lured me to music- creating something from nothing.

It is possible to serve two mistresses if you properly respect each and devote yourself equally to each. Better even if the mistresses become friends and serving one is also serving the other. To know what goes on behind the scenes of digital media is to imagine the full flower of both the code and the output.

Coke

It was super late when Joel rolled in sporting the usual stained linen Fanucci suit dragging a large plastic suitcase. Which obviously contained some quantity of drugs. After a few minutes of trad greeting rituals Joel began to glaze over and teeter about like one of those toys that are held together with elastic and go limp when you thumb the plunger. After many moments of old fashioned slo mo zombie-like behavior he pulled out a golf ball sized clump of silvery white cocaine from his baggage and told me to hide it from him, which I did in one of the vaults in the library ceiling. The next day he seemed to forget what he had exhorted and asked me to dole him out a 'little bit' of the stash which I did after making him go to another room. Over the next few days he hectored me to unhide it enough times that I returned him the remainder to manage himself. I am not sure at what pace he consumed it but I bet it was gone just about when it was time for him to move on to another mysterious caper.

Cocaine has never had the effect on me it has on most, which is why someone would trust me with their cocaine. I enjoyed putting a little on my gums and feeling my face go numb, but never liked snorting stuff up my nose and the snot made me feel like I was having a hay fever attack. And much like my involvement with other drugs, I kind of take my cues from the behavior of others under the influence. If they become sloppy or obnoxious, it doesn't necessarily mean I will. It just never appears to me to be as enjoyable as the hype, especially if there is apologizing the next day.

Apparently, we are naturally constituted to enjoy drugs. We have little holes in our nervous systems just waiting to suck in those molecules, however toxic they may be in the long run. Unfortunately, we have no method of gauging the number and type of receptors in an individual so you might know if you would, say, be a candidate for addiction to something in particular. I also know people who have no sensitivity to certain drugs, so she's pretty easy to get drunk but a complete waste of cannabis.

Notopia

We didn't know it was our last Utopia album when we started recording, but it soon became apparent. Kasim had already left the band once, hoping to start a solo career so there was already a fault line. Willie declared he was going to get into record production and insisted he should get a credit, even though he spent most of the sessions trying to learn how to program electronic drums instead of actually playing which made the process extremely joyless and slow. Roger began to vocally bitch about what a pain it was for him to come all the way across the Hudson for what were becoming ever less productive sessions. At one point Roger decided not to show up at all and we took it as an existential affront. He had already committed a lot of time to side projects like his music programming language and our general impression was that he was fed up and ready to move on, so we saved him the trouble of quitting and fired him. A week or so later we came to a truce so we could finish the record, figuring it was pointless to find a replacement if the band wasn't going to continue to tour anyway. Response to the final product was generally cool, many fans complaining about the stiffness and sterility of the programmed drums and what seemed like an overall lack of humor. Go figure.

While I hated the idea of firing Roger, I hated more how the esprit de corps had gone out of the band. At times it seemed like it was us against the world and it made us more determined. Suddenly it's us against each other and we don't remember what our purpose is. We're not making the money we used to and since I have other prospects I don't notice the panic in the band, the prospect that they could no longer survive on what we were generating unless we were willing to shed any principles we had and become something else. We couldn't, so we didn't. The end.

Breaking up a band can be as tragic as a divorce, perhaps even a death in the family. When the Beatles announced they were breaking up it was the end of an era, even though they always expected it would never last. Make up and stay together forever- that's what we wanted. Screw what you guys want! Screw the inevitable! You woke up and we're still dreaming... no fair.

Child

I was contacted out of the blue by Laura Nyro from her home in Danbury, Connecticut. She had been trying to get a new record started in her home studio and a parade of former collaborators had failed to get the project moving. A lot had changed in the 15 or so years when I first met her at the Dakota, a marriage, a son, a divorce, a change in sexual orientation. Still, it was an opportunity I had always hoped to have so I rode my motorcycle down to her place. We decided to focus on one song and work on it until it was done and chose To A Child as our starting point. I don't remember exactly what I did, but within a few days we had a take (amongst the many takes) and could move on to the rest of the record. As the sessions progressed the differences in our approaches to the process became more stark. We would record a take, she would say "That was nice. Let's try another one", until we had 2 dozen versions with microscopic differences between them, and no particular idea which was the best. TBD. Also, her girlfriend played percussion in the band and Laura depended on her opinion more than anyone's, despite the fact that she often played out of sync with the groove. At lunch time a coven of her lady friends would come over and sit around a table eating pizza, talking about how dietetically naughty they were, and make fun of men in general. I didn't take that very personally, but the snail's pace and the indecision were too much for me and I politely begged out of the project, one for which I would get no credit or thanks anyway.

I guess by the time I got to actually work with Laura we were both very much different people. I was once in awe of her passion which seemed to have cooled with age, while mine seemed to have broadened and deepened. Her musical world was growing smaller, over-emotionality was unseemly. I was trying to become a soul singer, liberate myself from self-consciousness. I left the project feeling that I had at least retired any outstanding fantasies and settled any karma that had resulted from her great influence on me.

Most people will never meet their idols and will therefore never be required to confront the humanity of someone that had previously occupied a mystical place in the universe. It's especially surprising to find that they may have the same insecurities and foibles as you and that can be a disappointment. We want to believe that the human condition can be transcended and transmuted by gods and goddesses that walk among us, human yet unattainable.

Saris

Joel, Kazi, Bean and I touched down in New Delhi just before dawn and after enduring the swarm of hacks and the dubious driving of our designee, arrive at our luxury hotel, one of a dozen incredibly grand constructions in an enclave surrounded by the institutional poverty that is typical. The Indian mentality has no problem with such juxtapositions. We get a couple of really big suites near the top and have cocktails as dawn breaks. New Dehli has comparatively little electrification and is covered with a blanket of smog from all the wood and coal that's burned. Still there are trees everywhere and very little urban noise reaches us. The air glows orange in the early rays and there is something almost eerily prehistoric and comforting about the scene, that the pace of evolution is measurably slower. We rest for a little while and decide to get into the thick of it, hopping a jitney to the old city. I still remember most of the points of interest from my previous trip so I lead everyone around the Red Fort and the palatial gardens and into the alleys of Old Delhi. Joel is fascinated by what can be gotten at the average pharmacy and decides to see what the street has to offer. "You want sari?" asks the street hustler. "You got hash?" asks Joel. Yes, he does have hash, grass and opium. We follow him to one of scores of narrow tailoring stalls, place a liberal order for contraband and then spend a half hour or so picking out fabrics and being fitted for pajamas and saris. The messenger returns with Tootsie Roll sized chunks of hash and O and a little bit of yellowish 'grass' that is probably more closely related to tobacco. We pay about 60 bucks for the clothes and drugs and head back to the hotel to plan our next move.

Every time I return to India I think I've gotten it, that I don't have to relive this, that I'll not be or at least won't plan to be back. That the chaos, the contrast, the backwardness and forwardness of it is an entertainment I no longer need. That my imaginings of the Mystical Kingdom have been resolved with higher reality and I can move on to the dissolution of some other glamour. And then I'll have a remembrance like the smokey orange dawn over Delhi and I'll be back at the threshold of a revelation that I could only experience in this place, and I dream of returning.

The pace of change will eventually reach the ends of the earth. We may resist some of it, but it is of a whole. You cannot have your Internet without the things it will reveal about the rest of the world and the people in it. Soon you will not be able to go to a place on earth that has resisted change the way that India has for so long. Not even in India itself.

Charmed

We had only allowed for a few days in India before moving on to Nepal and were holding more drugs than we could consume in a month. We tried to keep up but the jetlag and opiates simply made us unconscious so when it was time to go we still had most of our original purchase. Just before we leave for the airport Joel stuffs the stash in a Cadbury candy bar wrapper and hides it under his nuts. As we get to the gate there's a row of 'frisking booths' we have to pass through. Joel says don't worry about it but we find ourselves waiting in the lounge while a small commotion is occurring in Joel's booth, security streaming in from all directions. He peeks around the curtain and tells us to go ahead, he'll take care of it. We're sitting on the plane figuring out who's going to the embassy in Kathmandu to tell them about our busted friend in an Indian prison, and they're just about to pull the ramp away when we see Joel sprinting down the tarmac. He tells us they found his wad but that he had dropped some names and information, made a phone call and convinced them he was working for the CIA or Interpol or something and they let him go- with wad intact! I just don't know what to believe except that he is one charmed motherfucker.

When Joel got detained I thought "This is going to be like Midnight Express" and hoped that between me and Bean and Kazi we'd figure out a solution, although I'm not expecting much from either of them since I'm the only one who has been to Delhi before. I should have known that Joel was the wiliest of all of us. Or the luckiest.

How much trouble would Joel actually have been in for trying to smuggle hash and opium out of India and into Nepal? The question is ludicrous, of course. Only a decade before, Kathmandu was the worlds biggest hippie magnet because of its reputation as an open market where you could actually legally buy such drugs in a 'drug' store. The market closed up only because of pressure from western governments and in most of the Hindu and Buddhist and some Moslem enclaves enforcement was non-existent. Smuggling drugs to Kathmandu? Coals to Newcastle. The Delhi airport security was probably laughing their asses off at us.

Michele

After the release of Love Bomb we thought a Tubes/Utopia double bill would be a good ticket so we set out to tour together. Two weeks after the first gig the pricks at Capitol Records dropped the band. Nevertheless we all had a good time, Utopia becoming a part of the Tubes road routines- interior decorating the buses, hair dye parties, weird vocal warmups, etc. We were doing a show at a college in Michigan in a very traditional and pretty small area-wise venue with a Shakespearian raked stage. Our set was precarious but without incident. The Tubes, being much more an acrobatic performance, did not fare as well when one of the performers fell and struck her throat on something and had to be taken to the hospital. Fortunately, she was not seriously injured as demonstrated by her offer of exactly forty-five cents to someone who would arrange a tryst between her and I that night. Such bargain tryst did take place. Her name was Michele. She arranged to have a big flower arrangement for me upon checkout the next morning. I guess it was not much of a secret after that.

While I had never been strict about it, I always thought I had a type. You could simply look at someone and deduce that they were not your type. You might probe further and discover they may in some apocalypse be the perfect breeding partner but wow, how likely is that?

Men don't get sent flowers after a one night stand. If one ever does, one assumes one has done something spectacular even if one can't recall what it is. Having someone give you flowers is a great thing. I get it now.

Voices

Sound samplers were becoming all the rage so I got myself one called an Emulator. I had an idea to make a record using only my voice as a sound source and this would allow me to undertake that experiment. Beatboxing wasn't really a thing yet so I kind of experimented with various vocal noises and plosives at close range to the mic to simulate drum sounds and then play patterns on the Emulator keys because there were few midi sequencers. I resorted to a whole range of techniques to make the voice sound like other instruments. As the record, which came to be A Capella, progressed I opted for occasions of purity where voices were only voices. In the end I was pretty happy with the result and presented it proudly to Bearsville for release, the last record on my contract. Weeks later I hear nothing and ask Albert what the deal is. He says the record is unacceptable and he won't release it. I believe he is fucking with me because it's the end of the contract and try to hold out, refusing to even address the issue. Months later I demand to know specifically what the problem is and he says Warner Records has balked. I try to reach Mo Ostin to confirm this, finally reaching him from a phone booth on the Palisades Parkway. He tells me he has never heard the record and I realize Albert is Albert and sure enough, he will let me take my final record to Warners if he can have the publishing on my next 3 records. I took the deal and never spoke to Albert again.

The only class I ever truly loved in school was chorus, odd because I wasn't really that into vocalists at the time. I liked singing in the choir because nobody could really hear me but myself. The lessons I learned about breathing and pronunciation have been ingrained in me ever since. And what I thought was a very simple instrument turned into a lifelong fascination, something that, no matter how much I use it or think I know about it, keeps evolving.

Wandering minstrels still exist except they don't wander once they find a prime location in the subway. Their services are in far less demand nowadays since everyone is playing what they want to hear on their devices. But there was a time when music and musical talent were rare and at tuppence for a melody an engaging performer could make a pretty good living. Not quite enough of a living that you weren't still required to wander.

Francis

Somehow, probably because I built a video studio, I got invited to a confab organized by Francis Coppola at his house in San Francisco that was focused principally on cutting edge imaging and included not a few of the luminaries of a nascent CGI movement- creating images out of numbers instead of sets and actors. Miraculously, I had some insights that made my presence seem worthwhile and thus began a relationship of some sort between me and Francis. I guess he didn't associate with a lot of pop musicians and meeting an actual one that knew something about something was intriguing. I went once to see him speak at Montreux and introduced him to Claude Nobs, European head of Warner Records and organizer of the Montreux Festival. He was presenting a lecture about his creative process and whether he used the term 'progressive refinement' in the course of the presentation, I don't recall. but that is what stuck in my mind ever since. Years later when I moved the family to the Bay Area we would regularly visit him at the Zoetrope building and dine with him at Tosca. He liked to cook- watched him make a pizza in a North Shore bistro and make pasta with calamari at his 5th Avenue pied a terre- and we got along pretty well. Years on we got invited to a crowded event at the vineyard and whatever connection Francis and I may have had seemed suddenly imaginary. I did hear from him once a few years later when he personally reached out to see if I had any influence over my publishing company to help Sofia get a favorable license for some of my music, which I did happily. Never made it onto the soundtrack album.

I was never a real film buff but there were certain names you had to know, and Coppola was one of them. But for all his successes, the most important thing to him was family and I totally got that. He was like an uncle to my kids and he seemed to enjoy their company at least as much as mine. Maybe that's what we really had in common, and why we lost our connection.

Progressive refinement doesn't really sound like a novel concept and it's surprising how few creators use it. Performing arts are usually broken down in discrete steps: write the script, cast the actors, shoot the picture, edit the result. Each step costs money and time and you don't know what you have until all steps are completed. Imagine if you are always writing, always shooting, always editing. Start with a piece of butcher paper and draw out an arc, then start sticking bits of dialog on it, pictures clipped from magazines, photographs of the actors. Don't like what you've written? Replace it. Film a read of the scene, then replace it with final footage. Move things around if you think of a better arc. All the while refining every aspect of the product. Sounds easy unless you've never considered it.

Randy

Even though having Rex was a radical change from a lifestyle of complete irresponsibility, Bean and I felt we were good enough at child creation and maintenance (and since she had apparently forgotten whatever discomfort was involved) we set about to knock her up once again. Bean went into labor early in the afternoon and Randy was born about 1AM weighing in at 13 pounds, the biggest baby delivered all year at the hospital. Once again, Bean was remarkably poised through the whole thing- we spent most of the labor watching sitcom reruns on the TV in the birthing room. He was an eternally happy baby, slept much better than Rex and like Rex, never crawled- he was walking at 6 months. When he began to talk he realized he had no middle name so we let him pick one: Ninja Turtle. We had a Lhasa Apso that we also let him name: Fruit Stand, later to be renamed Michael Jackson. He got a bad stomach flu when he was less than two and couldn't keep anything down, but he was so cheery all the time we had no idea how sick he was until he started having convulsions from dehydration. He smiled all the way to the emergency room.

Bean and I both wanted a little red-haired girl as a second child but we weren't disappointed when Randy became a big enough fetus to tell he was a boy. As soon as we knew I declared his name would be Randy, after my recently dead friend, and Bean didn't seem to mind- as we all know fights can break out over baby names. I think she liked the alliteration: Rex and Randy Rundgren has a righteous ring to it. Names for an author or a sexy TV doctor. Or a baseball player.

The biggest problem with dogs is that they don't actually know their names. They know that there's a sound you make when you want a particular dog's attention, but they don't think "Blue, that's me!" Or "Yeller, that's him". You will discover this if you are foolish enough to adopt two stray dogs from the shelter. You want the dogs to respond to different sounds, or 'names', and think that by looking at one of the dogs and repeating the sound the dog will remember its name. But it doesn't matter which dog you are looking at, both of the dogs are thinking "Who me? You're not talking to me are you?". You get one dog, which bonds to you and pays attention to you and eventually recognizes the sound you make when you want its attention. Then you get the other dog. Having said that, human kids are often easier if you have more than one and they will be able to respond to the question, "What's your name?"

XTC

I woke up one morning at the Sunset Marquis and two things happened. One was horrible- a rocket full of astronauts had exploded. The other was a call about the possibility of producing XTC. I was a fan but also well familiar with the history of the band so while I eagerly accepted, I also girded my loins for what I knew could be a challenge. I spoke first with their A&R man at the label who informed me that the band needed a successful record or they'd be dropped. Then I spoke with Andy Partridge, the assumed leader of the group who expressed that they didn't really have a concept or direction, just a bunch of songs. I had him send everything they were considering and between Andy's songs and the unusual spate of composition from Colin Moulding I found a lot to consider. I decided I would try to apply some of Francis' progressive refinement technique and began to find photographs that represented each song. For instance, I found a picture of a riotous English garden with its haphazard plantings of pink and purple blooms which became the visual template for Drowning In Summer's Cauldron. We made the song sound like the picture looked, fleshing it out with natural noises in subtle sync, bird twitters and dog barks in rhythm. Every song had an image, a dark factory, a sunny beach, a sacrificial bonfire. The running order was a song cycle, morning to evening, January to December, birth to death.

Despite our agreement to abide by my concept, something perverse in Andy caused him to challenge it. We rerecorded a demo called Another Satelite, not because it fit into the song cycle but to simply mollify and humor Andy. Though there were challenges throughout the project, this turned out to be the most joyless exercize, something that in the end only satisfied Andy and otherwise stuck out like a sore turd in an otherwise near-perfect listening experience.

A record producer is not the same as a film producer. Movies are notorious for running over budget and spawning feuds between studios and auteurs. The producer in that context is the final sayso in any conflicts, but doesn't necessarily concern himself with creative. A record producer technically works for the artist, since the fee will be charged against their royalties. Most labels and artists don't even grasp this simple relationship and often the producer is in the middle carrying water for both sides. In the end you do what's right for the artist, even if everybody wants to fire you for it.

Frisco

In 1985 we moved to San Francisco, Lake Hill's horrible winters, stunted social life and spartan school options making the move pretty painless. Things seemed to fall into place, Bean having a 'richer' social life, me being where the cyberaction is and the kids, for better or worse, growing up in a major metroplex. We found a place on Chestnut Street off of Columbus Avenue in the North Beach district, right next to the San Francisco Art Institute. There was a huge used furniture warehouse on Broadway whence we acquired in a few chairs and sofas and beds and a pulpit which became the hifi station. We also snagged a nearly new car, a TV and cable account within a week and it looked like we were settled in. I interleaved all this with XTC sessions at Cave Canum (Latin for "sound hole") the studio we built to complete the recording of the Tubes 'Love Bomb'. The move didn't seem to have much affect on the pace of recording. To the contrary, a new batch of players seemed to revitalize the project, especially getting some real drums from Prairie. Even in the swirling chaos of the transplant I was able to churn out orchestral charts for the project. Everybody seemed happy.

I hadn't realized the degree to which life in Lake Hill had stunted my musical growth. In NYC I had collaborators of all kinds at Secret Sound, but the more folky/country leanings of the Upstate players didn't inspire me a lot, which didn't have a great effect on my output but also didn't encourage me to get out of the studio and mingle. By the mid-Eighties my hermetic adventures were starting to feel automatic and I could feel it was time to shake things up. I wasn't fully familiar with the Bay Area scene but I was ready to find out.

I have always maintained that isolation is a good thing for creativity, the opportunity to block out the noise and immerse yourself in your own thoughts. That said, it's not the best formula for a young family. There is a difference between sharing a home together and being trapped with one another. I'm imagining that little house on the prairie a month into a winter blizzard and no TV or stereo and you've read every book and listened to every story and the next thing you know there is blood all over the dirt floor.

Colin

Skylarking was a particularly painstaking production, what with Andy's perfectionism and the part by part layering process. Moving the project to San Francisco helped relieve the claustrophobia of my cramped control room and brought in a fresh set of personalities which created a little breathing room between me and the band. Most of the time was spent overdubbing Prairie's drums and bringing in session players for the more orchestral numbers. When we got to Earn Enough For Us it was decided to take a crack at a live performance- the only song on the entire album when the band all played together. Suddenly we all got a glimpse of XTC before Andy's stage fright, jangley and rollicking and everyone was euphoric after we captured it in less than 5 takes. We all went home feeling pretty satisfied with the session. The next morning I came into the control room to find Andy and Colin already at work. Andy was making Colin punch in every other phrase to conform to what his performance would have been if Andy dared to take over the bass, which he would gladly do. As a fan and producer, I offered that there was nothing wrong with the live performance, arguing it represented a rare glimpse of the band in the raw. Andy, with his usual flair for language, offered that he would like to cleave my head with an axe. Things became heated while Colin sat by until he suddenly stood up and declared that he was done, with the record and the band, storming out and leaving us in silence.

After Colin declared he was fed up with everything and everybody I had a pretty hard time convincing myself that I had somehow precipitated this potentially catastrophic episode, but I was in some small way relieved. At least I wasn't the only one confronting Andy for a change. Up until then nothing seemed to humble him and I was easily cast as the bad guy. Suddenly it wasn't simply my will against his. If we ever got Colin back in the studio I would be in an improved position.

When Andy said he wished to axe me it didn't come off as an actual threat. It was, however, an insight into someone who saw me as a threat. You think you are trying to serve your stated purpose, but to one you are serving you become an existential threat. When I signed on to the project, I didn't realize it would eventually lead to open fantasies about my bisection. But when it did a distinct Briticism came to kind: In for a penny, In for a pound.

Hackers

Shortly after moving to San Francisco I was invited to the Hacker's Conference. It was the third year of what is now a tradition of several decades and represented a breakthrough in terms of attendance and visibility. It took place at a Jewish summer camp in the hills of Saratoga. People would point at a distant peak and say "That's Neil Young's spread." I got to the site fairly early on Friday for the weekend-long event to an already well populated panoply of all manner of geeks, nerds, dweebs and geniuses the likes of which have inspired so many dumbed-down movies and TV series. There are guys who invented the first microchips, who have jobs for the government that they can't talk about who drive recumbent bikes with solar powered cellular espresso makers that will one day head multi-billion dollar corporations. I was assigned a cabin with 3 other bunks in it and which I would barely see the inside of for the duration. I had no idea what to expect but I had my Mac with me to show off what I was working on (and did so at every opportunity) and a head full of theories that often conflicted with other popular memes and encouraged the kind of fervid bantering that characterized the backdrop of the conference. You never knew what people might be arguing about and half the time it would sound like a foreign language. There was a 24 hour open bar and three good squares a day in a great hall that became impromptu science lab during the late hours (at one point I witnessed a demonstration of anti-gravity). Since so many participants worked and lived in the area the head count swelled from about 200 at the Friday evening opening presentation to 500 by Saturday night. I heard and met many of the inventors of computers, many younger people who would soon become household names and many who would soon head some of the most important companies that would fuel the computer revolution. Out of 48 hours I must have slept 5 and left on Sunday with a head abuzz with ideas and a shitload of valuable connections.

It was a revelation to be among so many people thinking about and talking about what had possessed me for so long. That thing I had spent so many solitary hours studying and which occupied so much of my thought. The infernal machine that had become a constant companion, challenging me to try to control it, to figure out how to communicate with its alien intelligence. All of the constant rumination that made no sense to my family and for which they had no interest. Suddenly I am among others who ruminate on the same ideas and are equally misunderstood by their friends and family.

Genie in a bottle- that's what a computer is. If you only understood how to talk to it, without complaint it would do your bidding regardless of how fantastic your expectations. If only you could figure out how to communicate with the dumb ass mutherfucking pseudo-personality that you have been making desk space for or lugging around the planet and recharging and tech supporting and growing ever more dependent upon. Don't you wish you could, well... hack through the obscurities and take control of that genie, speak to him in his own language? You know, be a hacker?

Chance

While we're on tour Michele and I live like a couple even though everyone knows that I will return to Bean and the kids when it's over. We're about to go do an A Capella show at The Chance in Poughkeepsie and I get a call from Bean on the pay phone backstage. She has heard about Michele and me and I admit that what she's heard is true. She demands that I end the relationship and I refuse. Moments later I'm onstage. We all spend the next week or so in limbo, not sure what the next move is. Bean realizes that her behavior has opened the door to this but hasn't really committed to changing it. I've made it clear to everyone that I am not leaving my kids, even if it means Michele and I may remain separated. Ironically it was Bean who broke the stalemate: invite Michele to come live with us. And as un-ideal as it was for Michele, her love for me and the kids prevailed and we all entered into the unknown.

I thought it was pretty obvious that the rules of my relationship with Bean had changed when she began parading her girlfriends around the house. It wasn't like we didn't love each other but there was no physical intimacy any longer and how long was I supposed to endure that? I am never leaving her and the kids to fend without me, and she must have sensed my unhappiness and took pity on me. I had never imagined an experimental family unit, but I had no trouble adjusting to it- likely a much easier time for me than the moms. Our greatest collective challenge was how to describe our household to the curious.

When you have children you have moved the center of your universe toward them. Whether by conscious desire or instinct your first thought should be of them. Even if you are not sure about how you feel about your offspring because you have taken the creation of a new life so idly, you are in them, they are the ultimate legacy. To abandon them is to lop off your branch of the tree.

Sunshine

We discovered fairly quickly that our landlord on Chestnut Street had a particular kind of tenant in mind and a noisy combination of kids and party people was not it and since we had the further prospect of two separate adult relationships in the same abode it was time to move out of the city. Somehow we found the ideal arrangement in Sausalito across the Golden Gate Bridge- two houses on the Banana Belt connected by a single door. We went through a couple of experimental arrangements and finally settled on Bean and the boys in the 'lower' house and Michele and I, my studio and eventually Rebop's nursery in the 'upper' house. Most family activity took place on the upper house ground floor where we had a large living and dining room and fairly ample kitchen. Daily life became a rotating routine of driving Rex and Randy through rush hour to their respective schools which seemed never to be near each other and attempting normalcy at the dinner table and the subsequent torture of homework, which I always felt hypocritical enforcing since I had done so little of it myself while in school. We had views of the entire bay from Tiburon to Alcatraz to Fisherman's Wharf. All in all, we were as happy as we could be under the circumstances at 69 Sunshine Avenue.

I am thinking this arrangement may yet work out. The most difficult challenge was explaining to curious others that I was living with two women and what the difference in our relationships are. Admittedly I am not completely sure. I suspect that it is not the love of me that has encouraged them to accommodate a situation that is equally challenging for both of them, especially to justify to their own parents and relatives. Pretty sure it was love of the boys that kept things together.

There is a distinct difference between fathering and husbanding. A lot of men opt for one at the expense of the other. For that matter, mothering and wifing are equally different and challenging skills. You love your children unconditionally, even as you are angry or disappointed in them. Grownups don't get off so easy when they don't live up to each others expectations. Then again, children are the result of an intimacy you had that they now actively interfere with. There is no winning, just trying to keep everyone happy and the damage to a minimum.

Blinn

The Hackers Conferences combined with the fact that I was a working musician enabled me to befriend a lot of ubergeeks, some of which were very uber indeed. Like our friend Ron who worked for NASA and would arrange flight simulator parties, or Jared who got crazy money out of people for VR products that never got out of beta, to real scientists doing crazy envelope exploding tech. That's how I met Jim Blinn, the father of CGI. Hard to recall nowadays, but there was a time before Star Wars when the big money was spent by the government to turn streams of numbers from satellites flying through the solar system into actual pictures. I visited him one time at Cal Tech where he had his lab and I was surprised to see that there were no rooms full of super computers, just a handful of PDP minicomputers. I got to be friends with him and at one point introduced him to Francis Coppola, hoping that might spark some scheme to fast track CGI into the commercial film making process. I also learned that he played trombone and years later had him on the session for The Want Of A Nail- you may even be able to pick out the trombone part in the arrangement.

You've got to be pretty fly when the things that come out of your head become 'models', the way that everyone imagines a painting or drawing before they put the brush to canvas. When I first saw Jim Blinn's work I recognized it but had little understanding of the underlying principles, defining distances and shapes, applying motion and mapping textures. At that time almost nobody did unless you attended one of the few schools that specialized in this budding field. And as previously noted, school and I have had a very rocky relationship in the past.

When you witness some modern spectacle of imaginary interstellar conflict depicted in billions of pixels generated by trillions of calculations, it is still wondrous that a single mind turned streams of numbers into the equivalent of the mind's eye flying through the solar system and establishing the foundation for all the pixels that followed, while also being a pretty good trombone player.

Flowfazer

We were out to dinner with some friends and their acquaintances and I struck up a conversation with a guy named Dave Levine. He had big crazy red hair like Sideshow Bob and brash opinions and a sense of humor and we got into some deep water over programming. He knew about the graphic tablet software I had written for Apple and said he was working on something I might be interested in. It was a program that essentially created what looked like a digital lava lamp, which he explained was actually a representation of magnetic nodes interacting with each other. I didn't much care about that, it just looked really cool and we decided to make a screen saver of it. Dave was used to getting way down deep into the code and I was into building interfaces so it made a convenient division of labor. Dave came up with the name Flowfazer- he really liked alliteration in his project names, and after a few months we had a product. We introduced it at MacWorld intending to publish it ourselves. As it turned out we had some heavily funded competition in Berkeley Systems Flying Toasters, but we did create a splash. The big drunken party at a Mexican restaurant helped a bit. We probably could have made a lot more money if we had ported it to Windows but we so loathed the platform that neither one of us wanted to make desk space for a cruddy PC.

Before Flowfazer all of the software I had worked on was in the 'mad scientist' methodology, grand ideas that usually don't make it out of the prototyping stage and are never released commercially. Think Professor Frink from the Simpsons, one crazy concept after another that never makes it to market. While it was kind of satisfying to finally get a product out, marketing was never my forte and I would soon be off on some other potential development that might change the world or more likely be a waste of time.

I am not very sophisticated mathematically and maybe that is why computer programming appeals to me. In the end you are dealing with bits and bits are just patterns not numbers. I have much awe for people who do understand the rarefied disciplines of calculus and number theory. I am a testament to the fact that there is too much math in school- I don't remember anything from trig, the class I needed to pass to get a HS diploma. I'm comforted by the fact that nobody remembers the math they were taught in grade school.

Macworld

About the time we moved to San Francisco, Apple Computer was becoming something of a phenomenon after the introduction of the Macintosh line, enough so that the Moscone Center could be filled with enthusiasts and peripheral and software manufacturers. There were always a surprising number of one-man shops with some left field mouse replacement or word processor or screen saver. Since musicians had yet to fully focus on the possibilities of computers, I got a lot of recognition and free stuff just wandering around the floor. And the parties were the best- and we gave the best parties. The first one we had was at our old apartment on Chestnut Street, where our friend from NASA brought a government computer that allowed us to track every flight that was in the air at that moment. Another year we had a bash at a graphic studio and that's when we started to get a reputation- " Are you guys throwing a party this year? Can I come?". It got to the point that all we had to do was print up a few flyers the day of the event and hundreds of people would show up. We kind peaked when we opened up the house at 69 Sunshine. The world showed up. There were engineers and CEOs and Francis Coppola in the kid's room getting a demo of the new Next machine. Soon the cops were at the door, and if you've ever met the Sausalito cops, they're the fucking worst. No more Macworld parties at 69 Sunshine.

It was still unusual in the late 80s for a pop musician to know anything about computers- maybe me and Thomas Dolby. He started a company that licensed a sound engine and more or less stopped making music. While I enjoyed making our little Grokware products, it had never crossed my mind to short change my musical career. I was thinking about different ways to present the music but I still wanted to make the music that got presented.

Most musicians do not play for life. If you've written a lot of songs that still get played you might 'retire' and live off the royalties, but that would be a small percentage of players. Many will stay in the business but essentially get a desk job like A & R or marketing, but that's probably a minority as well. That means that a whole bunch of players have had to find other jobs after spending their entire lives learning to do one thing. At least you're not likely to be replaced by a robot. Unless you're in Kraftwerk.

Broadway

I was contacted about writing music for the Public Theater. The project was based on an unfinished script by Joe Orton who was enjoying a posthumous revival via a successful run of "Loot" on Broadway. The PT had acquired an option to stage an unfinished script supposedly intended to be the Beatles third movie. Probably because I was a notorious B-boy and had done covers and entire tribute albums it was presumed I could and therefore would write the soundtrack to the movie that was never made. They were hoping to find something that would replace A Chorus Line, a cash cow for the Theater that was wrapping up its run on Broadway. Expectations were high and the investment was considerable by PT standards. We had a director and a choreographer of some notoriety, an arranger/conductor with a band of six multi-instrumentalists and a cast of at least 15. Tom Ross, the producer made an executive decision that everyone should speak with a British accent and since the one thing we didn't have was a dialog coach, the results were spotty and sometimes risible. That and the fact that none of the music sounded Beatley garnered the show tepid reviews at best, although it did get a Tony nomination for Alison Fraser's performance of Parallel Lines. My most vivid memory of the production was the night Michele and I attended a preview and during the intermission we got the news that San Francisco had been struck by a major quake.

The one thing I am sure I got out of my experience with the Pub was the opportunity to get to know Joe Papp. I was raw and he was avuncular and strove to educate me and indulge me and even in the midst of what seemed failure, encouraged me to think in even grander terms. I'm pretty sure a lot of others benefited as I did. Even as we were digesting the unenthusiastic revues Joe took me aside and asked me to think about writing an opera for the PT. Shortly thereafter he became ill and retired from the theater, leaving me without a champion and the project never realized.

Broadway is a far different animal than Off-Broadway. Broadway productions take years to mount and cost millions of dollars and anyone with a serious stake focuses on nothing else. Off-Broadway could be a one-person show with a 5 figure budget. Almost everyone involved has a regular job and is hoping move up to full-time entertainment at a decent salary. Many players will have minor or non-speaking roles in other productions and are hoping to pad their resumes and maybe get some recognition. It's hard to blame them if you don't get 100% concentration during rehearsals. Showbiz is just as hard as they say it is.

I got it into my head that I should start recording live in the studio since everything in pop music seemed overdubbed to death. For a couple months I would write and arrange during the week and call a session at Fantasy Studios on the following Sunday. The routine was pretty much the same for every song- call in the rhythm section and teach them the song, then take the singers to another room to learn the backgrounds while the band rehearsed, then run over the charts with the strings and/or horns, then mash it all together sometime by late afternoon. We would do takes until I was sure we had everything covered correctly then take a break whereupon we would get as drunk and high as quickly as possible before capturing the 'mood altered' performances that, as it turned out, made up the bulk of the final album. Ironically, the end result was a boost to my career and garnered the lead review in Rolling Stone. The tours that resulted fulfilled my dream of having a 'review', a big band with singers and horns and slick arrangements and we went around the world and slayed wherever we played. If it hadn't been so expensive to maintain I might have gone on for years with that approach, but my arrangement with Warner Brothers was coming to a close and that I meant I had no more record production budgets and no more tour support. I did manage one more crack at all-live recording on the following record Second Wind which was recorded at the Palace Of Fine Arts in front of a live audience, just to add excitement to the performances. I made them pretend they were in church so it would sound like a studio album.

Since I hadn't done many live recordings since Something/Anything I had forgotten the sensation of hearing the final product while you are capturing it. It's hard to describe- you are listening to the music that everyone will eventually hear coming out of your mouth in real time. I don't know if any of the other musicians experienced the same sensation but it was difficult at times not to be distracted, especially in light of how tedious and meticulous the process had sometimes become. There it was, complete and all at once.

There was a time when all music was recorded live and complete. Enrico Caruso sang opera to dozens of wax cylinder recorders at once because there was no way to duplicate the physical artifact. Not only were the performances unique for every batch of cylinders hollered into, but each had a different 'mix' because each occupied a different location relative to the performer. Even at 100 captures at a time, it would have taken 10,000 performances to create a million seller. The up side, I guess, is that piracy was unheard of.

Customs

We were crossing the border back into the Good Old USA when we got pulled over by customs at Port Huron. There were few agents at the crossover but one pint-sized Chuck Norris wannabe took a special interest in us. Scowling the entire time he barked orders at us like a drill sergeant and though we had scoured the bus for any contraband he made us all feel guilty of something. He and a couple other creeps went through the bus with a fine tooth comb and managed to find a 2" piece of plastic straw tucked into a fake flower pot, something left over from someone else's tour. That kicked Little Chuck into a whole other gear and we were all made to empty our personal effects. Wouldn't you know somebody had a skinny forgotten joint at the bottom of their bag and at that point the shit completely hit the fan. We are all subjected to strip search while they break out the power tools and begin disassembling the bus. In the end they have nothing to show for humiliating all the innocent but the skinny joint. We followed the police car with the 'perp' to the county courthouse, everyone shaken by the treatment we got from our own government over something we could have found within a mile of the border. I have since referred to the crossing as Port Urine.

It wasn't as if I had never run into a little prick empowered by the state before. Philly cops would pick me up for no reason, transport me to a far off station, have their fun with me then turn me back on the street to find my back to where they picked me up. I thought it all emanated from that Notorious Prick Rizzo, the mayor who was once the chief of police. But time has proven that this is a disease anyone could succumb to. Worse, an endless opportunity for revenge on the innocent by those who should not have passed the psychological evaluation. You think these are exaggerated characters from a movie until you run into one in the flesh.

As long as there are pricks in the world there are going to be jobs for pricks and the job that a prick most wants is fucking with other people, and the best place to fuck with other people is where people really need something, like getting back into their own country. The pretense is patriotism, yet at the most cowardly outpost. And if you are an especially big prick, apparently you get sent to the loneliest part of the system, that being the long boring border between us and our closest ally. If you ever have a choice, fly over these people and leave them to their bitter loneliness.

Toast

After Apple published my paintbox program I became more connected to the CG community and started attending SIGGRAPH (Special Interest Group on Graphics of the American Engineering Society) conferences. It was a terrific forum to meet the 'stars' of this very young science, usually at some fabulous party with an open bar. The signature event was the film show, highlighting all the latest developments to the oohs and aahs and cheering of a packed house of several thousand pixel nerds. The rest of my time would usually be spent wandering the convention floor looking at professional gear that I couldn't possibly afford. There were Crays and Wangs all vying to be the fastest computers in the world because computer graphics was like no other application in its demand for speed and storage. One convention late in the 80s changed all that for me. A relatively unknown company called NewTek had set up a standalone kiosk with monitors mounted high all around it and on the screens were film show quality CG as well as a video demo of the system's keying and titling capabilities conducted by a sexy redhead in a very tight outfit named Kiki. Upon closer inspection I see that the hardware is based on a single Amiga computer. While I'm nosing around I'm approached by one of the engineers who introduces himself: "I'm Brad Carvey, Dana's brother". I have an in! I immediately resolve that I am going to make a computer generated video with this stuff and I order 3 systems.

There is awe in not just seeing something for the first time, but in being the first to see it. The first time the film show had anything resembling real smoke the sense of awe in the room was palpable. At the same time we all new that the next year we would see something yet more awe inspiring. It gave you a feeling of prescience like you knew something was going to happen before anyone else did.

Memes that we take for granted start out as baby memes that are cute as the dickens. In the early days of the post-Beatles revolution in music everything was fun, anyone could play along and the whole world egged you on. Then the potential for fortunes to be made opened the door to the lawyers and investment bankers and a meme became an industry. The revolution in computing started out the same way, hundreds of little companies like bands and indie labels sprung up everywhere, the world was egging us on and the parties were the hippest and funnest until... lawyers and investment bankers.

I began producing the video for Change Myself with the 3 Amigas and Toasters and realized it might take me a year to render the whole thing so I sent a couple of seconds of animatics to Newtek. They responded by shipping me another 27 Toaster-equipped Amigas, necessitating the rental of an office space in 'downtown' Sausalito. This brought the rendering down to a matter of weeks, which left me challenged to keep up with the design aspect so I set out to find some assistance. There was a small network of people in the Bay area who were into bringing CG to the masses and that's how I met Gary Yost who was publishing 3D software for the Artari computer. He suggested I look up Till Kruger, a student at San Francisco Art Institute, ironically enough, right next to the place we originally had on Chestnut. He had a demo reel of some short animations and still renderings of dark Gothic themes but had a grasp of the basics and was familiar with Lightwave, the software that ran on the Toaster. He had come to the US years earlier as a German exchange student and aside from the few months in San Francisco had spent most of his time in Alabama. He spoke American English quite well, fortunately with neither a Southern drawl nor a comical Sergeant Shultz German accent. He didn't smile much and I had a hard time figuring out if he had a sense of humor or not. I outlined some stuff I wanted 'built' for the project and sent him off to work. Then he disappeared. About a month later he showed up, sorely chastened, admitting he had been in a weird place and returned to Germany to get straightened out. Reluctantly, I gave him another shot. Glad I did.

I don't take it well if someone commits something to me and then doesn't deliver, especially if they give you no warning, no opportunity to find an alternative. I've held grudges for years, excommunicating the offender and avoiding situations where I might encounter them. Part of it is pettiness, I'm sure. But often I'm on some deadline and if they don't deliver, I can't deliver. And I'm very anal about delivering.

The world is full of people, whole cultures sometime who do not take commitment seriously. "Oh, get over it," they say. It's a great precedent to establish if you want to avoid responsibility in the future. Then some day you desire to be taken seriously because you have a real contribution to make. Or maybe there's a special reward you've always wanted. Then you find out how hard it is to build a history, a resume that never existed.

Nutopia

After I finished Change Myself I sent a copy to Newtek and was invited to come to Topeka to visit their headquarters, where I got official face-to-face intros to Tim Jennison, Paul Montgomery, Kiki Stockhammer and pretty much every one of the dozen or so employees. They had developed a corporate culture based in part on the mutual antipathy that festered between the town and the company, resulting in a purposefully oddball environment. It was the anti-tech tech company. The next morning Tim and Paul took me to a diner on the way to the airport and there they popped the question: would I like to partner with them to convert all those Toasters into a real studio and start pushing the possibilities of their products? Since I was already doing it it seemed like a no-brainer. I hired Till and we moved everything to another office in the same redwood Sausalito complex, mostly trying to figure out how the pile of computers should be compacted and networked. The Amiga hardware that held the Video Toasters was about as crappy as could be manufactured and it was a constant battle keeping a majority of them working. The chassis were crudely stamped and folded out of sheet metal whose raw edges would invariably slice up your hands every time you opened one to jiggle the cards or clean the contacts, leaving blood stains behind on every machine. We spent most of our time creating demos for the quickly evolving Lightwave software, which essentially guided the feature set: You want motion blur? Couple days for that. Lens flare? Easy, tomorrow. We would slave for a month 24/7 to render a 3 minute movie that would be debuted at company parties during SIGGRAPH. In the end it was difficult getting paying projects. Movie people did not take a studio based on Amiga computers very seriously.

Ever since I saw that first digital paintbox at NYIT I wanted to get into CGI and studied all the literature and attended all the conferences and conventions to make sure I knew what the latest developments were. In those days a lone hobbyist could get his head around the concepts enough to produce what looked like an industry standard piece of work. If I were to get into it today I'd likely only be scratching the surface of concepts that were unheard of when the Video Toaster was new.

The modern analogue to "Be careful what you wish for" would be "Be careful what you imagine". We have an ever increasing ability to realize what we imagine, even the horrible, like atomic weapons. We can now render with complete physical and optical accuracy the equivalent of pixel-powered visual vomit- Transformers.

Japanese

The US economy got so bad in the late 80s that the Japanese started buying a lot of American property to the consternation of many Yankees. The upside was that everything else American was suddenly affordable and attractive and that included American performers and record producers. The boon for me was twofold: not only could I afford to take the 11 piece Nearly Human revue on more than one Japanese tour, but I was being approached by Japanese artists to produce records there and in the US. My first project was for singer-songwriter Hiroshi Takano who was signed to a label founded by a member of YMO (THE proto-synth band). The studios in Japan had the most advanced equipment and biggest rooms and even the soundproof doors probably each cost thousands of dollars. We did two sides of a single in Tokyo and the rest of the album in Lake Hill, which must have been a shock for Takano since the doors in my studio are just doors and the control room is a small attic. The best part for me was getting to 'live' in Tokyo for a while and spend time with my hosts on their turf. I became fascinated with the culture, the grandiloquent architectural expressions, the attention to detail, the social mores that also indulged a certain desire to get crazy, like the Twisting Elvises of Yoyogi Park. There were still generations that had grown up while Douglas MacArthur was running the country so a significant segment of the city population spoke some English, especially in the service sectors. It was a great time to be in the capitol- I never could have indulged it but for the weak dollar.

Previous lives, should such exist, hold little fascination for me. But experiencing Japanese culture outside of a business context resonated in so many ways it's worth wondering why. The coexistence of nature and technology is of course appealing but feeling comfortable around people who speak a language so different from mine is something of a breakthrough. And I've always had loyal fans there who treat me like a family member, so that's probably a big part of that soft spot. Yet...

Well, because Japan is like, Japan. There is no other place in the world remotely like it. All the weird stuff that happened to it made it unique beyond compare. The isolation, the incredible confluence of natural beauty, the cultural cohesiveness... the bombs we dropped on them. You couldn't design a more perfect country Such a shame about that Pearl Harbor thing. Still, we are the best of friends.

Youngblood

Tim and Paul from NewTek called me and said I should meet them at SFO because we were going to take a chartered jet to Monterey for dinner. They brought along a fresh young face out of computer college named Eric Myers, a very smart and eager Toaster afficionado that they wanted me to consider as a Nutopia hire. Eric had much more hard-core experience and education than either I or Till so it seemed like a good idea. He was affable and eager and a bit daring as he had left a safe job working at his father's company, a big manufacturer of advanced micro-devices and that likely he would have one day wound up running. The first thing he did at the studio was figure out how to network the 30 or so Amigas together, something probably no one on the planet was trying to implement since there was not another such collection of cheesy hardware being put to some serious use. In time he began to reveal his other talents and got much more involved in the creative possibilities. Our friends became his friends, he became a regular at the compound volleyball games, he and Till became best friends, bonding over the torture I would put them through at the video studio. The Borg had assimilated him.

Rex was not yet a teenager and had yet to focus on a direction so it made me feel somewhat avuncular overseeing an enterprise primarily staffed with people who could be my children at a different stage of life. I remembered how I was always comfortable watching older men do their work, especially if they assumed I had the smarts to understand what they were doing. And while I hadn't the formal training that Eric and Till had, it was acknowledged that I had the experience and with that, the authority to establish our priorities. Nutopia could have been Rundgren & Sons Boutique Grafique.

For most of us there is no exact moment at which we pass into adulthood- it just sort of sneaks up on you. You wake up every day feeling as young as you ever did until the day you wake up feeling old and wondering where that came from. In a more kindly scenario you still feel just as young but you look around you and everyone is decades younger. Then you realize you are the adult in the room, the one who's expected to know what to do next. You always thought you would celebrate adulthood and now that it is on you you're horrified at the responsibility and saddened that your youth is officially a thing of the past.

Since I had been messing with computers a lot and had some inkling of what they were capable of, I got it into my head that there might be a different way to present the content. I started by experimenting with a tool that let me describe a list of sound clips and play them seamlessly and began demonstrating the concept at various conferences. Eventually I was approached by someone representing Philips who were looking for unique apps to support their new CD-i (Compact Disc Interactive) format. I got together with Dave Levine and we devised a system that allowed a listener to navigate a library of sound clips in real time and set up conditions for an 'intelligence' that would select clips automatically. We invented algorithms for 'gaussian randomization', a concept we were pretty sure was original but we had no time to research. Shortly after we delivered the final product Philips began to phase out the format so we ported it to Apples and PCs, a historically tortuous process especially on the Microsoft side since every PC was a random collection of junk hardware and crap system software. Suddenly we were in a nightmare world of customer support… "What is your OS version, which CPU, how much memory do you have, is the computer plugged into the wall, have you ever used a PC before?" That pretty much took the fun out of making products so I went back to making regular old records and Dave moved on to some programming arcana that only he could comprehend.

Up until No World Order I had been pretty anal about what the audience was supposed to experience from my records. It was a revelation to confront the fact that they were looking for a more granular way to absorb media, one that conformed to the new age of portable devices. The likelihood that a listener was going to surrender to my version and how it should be absorbed was becoming undependable and I had to accept that. Now if I could just get the music business on that wavelength. Naive.

When one sees a film or listens to a record or reads a book one is unaware of the options available to the creators and what informs the choices they make. You assume when experiencing something for the first time that it was always meant to be that way- what other way could it be? In reality, decisions are being made all the way up to delivery of the product about the best order to put things in and what should be expanded or removed, and even then some authors aren't satisfied and continue to revise… thus the dreaded Director's Cut.

Showdown

We began to suspect that Bebe was trying to make a living off of Liv and decided we should pursue custody. It seemed that much of the voluntary child support we were providing was being diverted to Bebe's lifestyle and that Liv might become a bargaining chip. Almost the moment we stopped the cash flow Bebe revealed Liv's true lineage. We demanded a paternity test, knowing what the result would be. Suddenly she was no longer a Rundgren- she was a Tyler (a lot easier to spell, I must admit). Liv embraced her new family and we did not hear from her for years after that. She became a successful model and then an actress so we would see her image everywhere but would never communicate with her. People, the press would want know the story but we all remained mum about it.

Mixed feelings? Fuck yeah. It wasn't accepting Liv as my daughter for 13 years, that was a special blessing that I may not have fully recognized, it was accepting Bebe as her mother. Enduring the endless manipulations, the obvious lies, it was no surprise when she saw it was time to cash in. Now we had to accept that Liv was not our girl, that we had been swapped out for another family. That we had been prepared to wake up with her every day and now there was only silence.

Sometimes you may struggle for years to figure out what the right thing is and try to adhere to it. Then you discover you have no power against those who have never confronted such struggles or striven to substitute anything but self interest as the goal. You may feel as if you have lost to something that proves your struggle isn't worth it. That's when you get drunk and get over it. It's the right thing to do.

Nightmare

For some stupid reason we wound up premiering the NWO tour in Japan. With all the technological details and constant programming, the prep began to creep into my unconscious life and I started to have literal nightmares about not being able to put all the pieces together. Compounding was the fact that someone had miscalculated the shipping cost and everything suddenly had to be on a boat two weeks earlier than planned which meant a lot of last-minute kludging and no chance to actually rehearse. Sure enough, when the show is unpacked in Tokyo almost nothing goes well. There is not enough juice to power everything, that juice being a different flavor so it would take an army of electricians to figure it out. I am in my room frantically trying to convince MAX, the programming language upon which the show is based, to cooperate. I get to the venue, a black hole in Shibuya, and behold a scene of utter chaos. While the stage seems to be properly assembled, half of the equipment won't start and crewmembers are defying electrocution whenever they touch a piece of metal. Outside the crowd has gathered in a persistent drizzle, some from as far away as Hiroshima, while we scramble until an hour after doors and decide to let everyone in to see what they are going to miss. I play 4 or 5 acoustic numbers over a sound system that is screaming an ungrounded hum and refund everyone. We take the better part of a week dealing with the worst issues and premier the show where we never should have.

I had constant nightmares while mounting the NWO show. There was so much detail between the video and lights and computers all talking to each other that my mind never gave up trying to balance everything on the head of a pin and that would have been enough to disrupt my sleep. But compound that with the fact that I had never performed anything like this before and I achieve a level of anxiety that lasted literally years after that tour left the road.

There is probably some foundation to dream interpretation, but I've never bothered to study it. Simple things you experience have a deep psychology behind them and things are usually symbolic of other things. But my nightmares of unpreparedness, almost always a variation of the living nightmare I experienced, are exactly what they seem- I am petrified of being caught with my pants down.

Interactive

I got approached to develop a music application based on No World Order for an interactive television experiment that Time Warner Cable had undertaken in a suburban Orlando neighborhood. I flew down to the Boca Raton headquarters for a bit of indoctrination then drove out to a demo house. The set-top box was an SGI Indigo computer, a souped-up graphics workhorse about the size of a rolling suitcase than might more accurately be called a set-crusher. Aside from on-demand movies, there was an application that let you order a pizza and specify the toppings and beyond that, not much that would justify the giant processor. I came up with a new, simplified interface and Dave Levine and I were ready to implement- all we needed was some real music that people would want to hear and put it on a server. Eric Gardner set up meetings with the special products divisions at the major labels and we set about to convince them to help us in what was then an experiment in on-demand music services. To one degree or another every label refused to even entertain the idea including, ironically, Warner Records. They all equated the concept with file sharing, a fad that they had not figured out how to deal with, and were horrified at the idea that music was being downloaded in any sense. A year later the concept became moot when the Time Warner Full Service Network project shut down and two years later Napster went online and what labels and artists wanted didn't matter anymore- it was all about what the audience wanted.

I was never positive that streaming music would substantially replace the CD. I thought it was more about programming music for a particular circumstance, rather than listening to an album or song because that was what you specifically wanted to hear. Since I had made the only interactive music product then or since, I didn't know what the experience of navigating someone else's music would be like or how a user might design a program for exercising or having dinner or sex. I'm still curious about what's possible.

The whole idea behind interactive media is that you can't predict what people want so you give them as many options as you think they can handle. But the other factor is the gamut of attitudes about what qualifies as interactive- not everyone wants to drive the car. The Holy Grail has become systems smart enough to 'sense' what you want. Your only decision is how much you desire to be babied by a bunch of code with the voice of your mother.

Rebop

Rebop was supposed to be born in an Edenic calving suite at Marin General, as one might expect. As Michele entered the third trimester she began to get really cranky, which is probably not unusual. She was also having flu-like symptoms so when her ob-gyn told her it might be a bug we thence never suspected it was gestational liver toxemia, like any competent ob-gyn might. The next time she saw that 'doctor' she left Marin for San Fran General in an ambulance. I met her at the emergency ward and they took us to a plain recovery room on the maternity floor where somewhere down the hall a woman was screaming bloody murder nonstop. They give Michele petosin to induce labor and start running tests on her, the most horrific of which was driving a needle into her wrist to collect arterial blood, and because somebody didn't get it to the lab before it coagulated, they had to repeat the sadistic procedure. Things seem like chaos with all the screaming and staff running around forgetting to deliver blood and such and the doctors finally realize that she is too weak for labor and they rush her into an operating room for a caesarian. Rebop is birthed nearly 10 weeks early and Michele is in a stupor for 3 days from the post-op drugs. He is about the size of a wiener dog puppy and has to remain in an incubator for over a week, his only contact with the family being my little finger.

I had been in the delivery room for all my other kids, even Liv. It was strange for me to be in the waiting room having no idea what is going on and trying to push the fear and confusion out of my mind. I'm used to being there to encourage and support and generally stay cool. Now I am in a stew of bad possibilities: will we lose the baby, will I lose Michele, maybe both? Why did it turn out this way, so different from what we planned? Our fate is in the hands of complete strangers.

Sometimes it's hard to trust doctors. It's like they don't know what they don't know. My experiences with medical professionals is so rife with misdiagnoses and misjudgments that I could produce at least a small booklet of horror stories. And hospitals are the worst. It's where all the sick people are. Check in with a hangnail and see if you don't check out with hepatitis or bird flu. The older you get, the more common it becomes to go in for something more or less routine and never leave because of endless complications. If you are lucky, and have anyone left to take care of you, you'll be released to hospice care and die without being connected to a pile of machinery. They'll probably boot you home anyway as soon as your insurance runs out.

Ringo

I signed on for Ringo's third incarnation of the All Starr Band but showed up a few days late for rehearsal because I was finishing up the abortive Utopia reunion in Japan. By then most all of the parts had been assigned to the other 3 guitar players (Joe Walsh, Dave Edmonds and Nils Lofgren) so I wound up doing a whole lot of acoustic guitar strumming. Aside from Ringo, the only other guy I had met before was Joe so there was much bonding to be done. That became more of a challenge after our first vocal rehearsal when someone suggested to Burton Cummings that he might be singing the wrong part which caused Burton to explode all over him. I knew then that Burton and I were destined to have a unique relationship. I was not aware of the proclivities of the various band members but it soon became apparent that there were 3 distinct camps: those who were in The Program, those who were definitely NOT in The Program, and the moderates of which I was one. Ringo was the leader of The Programmers, a group of about 8 players and crew members who had to have a meeting at least once a day. I remember seeing them on their way to one in Gothenburg, Sweden and imagining what the locals must have thought when Ringo shows up speaking Liverpudlian and they can't tell anyone! Joe and Burton were definitely NOT with the program. Joe was pretty discrete but Burton never seemed to plan ahead beyond emptying his minibar and then visiting everyone else's room and emptying theirs. He also had this 'gag' during American Woman where he'd lick the mic stand from bottom to top, which grossed us all out, prompting a series of experiments wherein we would smear something disgusting like an old shrimp or some hair product on the stand to see if he would notice- never did.

I'm not especially conscious of my reputation, but I made the assumption that everyone in the All Starrs at least knew something of the other players. Even Timmy Capello, the percussion/sax guy was familiar from his video appearances with Tina Turner. But Burton Cummings truly did not know who I was which annoyed him immensely. He was dumbfounded after visiting a record store in Kansas City and discovering that my bin of CDs was 'longer' than his. This was a special form of jealousy.

Music soothes the savage breast, but it doesn't necessarily make the musician a nice person. The angry exploits of Miles Davis and Van Morrison are legendary. You could say that music redeems the savage prick, but that prick better be able to play his ass off.

Vegas

It's Labor Day weekend and for the first time in years I don't give a shit about the Telethon. I am so happy to be ending the 3 month Ringo tour that on the day of the last show I begin consuming smoke and drink early and move on to mushrooms by mid-afternoon. By the time I get to Caesar's I'm feeling like one of Jerry's kids- the poster child. Someone has arranged for me to get into the wardrobe department and they suit me up like one of the centurions that wander the casino. I'm beyond giddy during the course of the show, especially when we go on air for the telethon- I launch into a fitful idiot dance that causes the plastic Martian helmet to gouge the bridge of my nose, leaving me bleeding and grinning Deliverance-style before they can cut away. I refuse to sit out the last rendition of 'American Woman', expressing every loathsome frustration I felt toward Burton like some kind of guitar humpin' Isadora Duncan. By the time me and Timothy B and his wife get back to the suburban trophy house I've been renting ("Cher stays there whenever she's in Vegas") things have truly peaked- it's like an Elvis movie with chicks frugging on the staircase and people going nuts in the pool and me commanding the white vinyl electric Barcolounger. Yeah, we got our money's worth that year.

It's hard to recall many of the fine details of that day, blizzard of enhanced experience that it was. There was a moment when I got back to the party that stands out as especially rich, the intensity of the collective enjoyment, guiltless and hedonistic that stood in such contrast to the previous three months. Even Timothy B noticed the thing that was now there that had been missing- a shared spontaneous hallucination of carelessness, of having nothing to battle against, no tribulations on the horizon. A noisy peaceful dream.

Every professional pop musician owes a karmic debt to the Beatles since most of us wouldn't have been in the business otherwise. I certainly paid mine off during those three months which puts me ahead of 99% of the players still left alive since 1964. That doesn't mean I could ever hold a candle to the Beatles. It's just that now I've finally got that giant Beatle off my back.

Wailapa

After a grueling couple of months at Nutopia cranking out a SIG-GRAPH demo I took everyone to Kauai for a vacation. Hurricane Iniki had flattened the island about 8 months prior and no hotels were open so we rented a couple condos in Princeville within eye-shot of the devastated luxury North Shore hotel. It looked like a giant blow torch had given the island a bad haircut, tree tops lopped off and piles of debris clumped like hair on a barber's floor. Our beloved Coco Palms Hotel, setting for Elivis' Blue Hawaii and the first place I ever stayed on the island was decimated beyond repair. We pretty much did what was left of the island in a couple days. Then I got it into my head that it would be an excellent time to go looking at property, figuring the market had to be rock bottom. Friends connected us to a realtor and we spent a couple days looking at raw acreage on the beach, jungle bungalows, giant inland plantations and McMansions and didn't get truly turned on by anything until the realtor suggested one last property. We drove down a long tree-lined lane and turned into the drive and saw for the first time the place that would years later become our home. Wailapa.

I was not the only one who had a visceral reaction to seeing the Wailapa site for the first time. If it had been a solitary hallucination I never would have gotten anyone else to buy into my obsession to live in this place. And while on first sight it was nothing but plowed under red dirt, imaginary temples sprung up wherever I looked. I immediately forgot about all the other exotic and spiritual places I thought I might retire to and committed thoughtlessly to that six acres.

There is a difference between feeling a connection to a place and truly building a connection. It's as serious as love and marriage. Your fervid love affair with a place can be just that- a fancy that cools or is replaced by a greater love for other places. Then you may find a place to commit to for life, through good and bad, sickness and health, unto death.

Patronet

In the early 90s almost nobody knew what the Internet was even though it had been around for a long time. Netscape, the first web browser was originally designed to display text, pictures and links to other pages. The first time I saw it was during a tour of Sun Microsystems when Bill Joy, one of the company founders, took us aside to show us how a 'web' page would appear on their setup and I was fascinated that the screen looked more like a printed page than a computer program. Most of the authoring was happening on college campuses since most of the content was scholarly. Soon everyone was imagining what they could do with this new communication platform and eventually the focus came around to making money. I was at a conference where most of the attendees were in the content business and trying to figure out how to monetize the net. I was supposed to speak but wasn't sure about what until it dawned on me that this platform would allow a creator to go directly to the audience for funding, rather than being loaned the money by a publisher. I thought it was such a good idea that I was afraid someone might steal it so I set about trying to implement the concept, calling it PatroNet. Web browsers had persistent problems with security and asset management so I designed my own protocol and built my own 'browser' and actually got a couple thousand subscribers, but the constant moving target of the technology and versioning for various platforms sucked away so much of my time that I was making less and less actual music. After almost a decade of fits and starts the project went into permanent limbo.

When I created I was not prepared for the kind of human behavior I would have to confront. I knew that there would be the typical 'customer service' issues to deal with, but there hadn't been a lot of similar situations where you could so easily interact with other users and it often brought out the worst in people. Fights would break out over who was the most authentic fan, flamers would upset the entire community with bilious screeds, creeps would trick members into thinking I was communicating with them. Pretty common now, but it was all new back then. It was a relief when it stopped.

Money changes everything. There was a brief window when the internet had some purity, things were there because they were worth knowing. Information that was historically hard to find became instantaneously accessible. Yes, there was nothing to stop you from publishing porn, but there was no profit motive. You simply did it for the love of porn.

Bankrupt

The owner of the 2 lots at the end of Wailapa Road was a prick. Even though Kauai was still in terrible shape and properties were up for sale all over the island he sensed how much we wanted the place and demanded over-market money and no paper, which we were not able to manage so we reluctantly put that dream to sleep. A year later Meatloaf decided to have Sony Records audited for unpaid royalties and asked if I wanted to get in on the act. I had no interest in getting involved in a protracted assault and offered him my points for cash. He demurred so I sold them back to Sony. Just for the hell of it we checked Kauai realty listings and Wailapa was available, both lots substantially reduced in price so we made the offer. Of course when Jerkwad found out it was us he claimed that there was a hold on one property and that we'd have to buy both at a price that was a year old. To further torture us he demanded a face-to-face with us wherein Michele conjured some discrete weeping and I was forced to walk him around behind the scenes at Woodstock II. We finally paid off the extortionist and took possession of our dream location. The next year was not a great moneymaker and coupled with the gigantic cash expenditure of the previous year the IRS was not happy. For more than a decade they had been coming up with new bills based on disqualified investments my accountants had made in the 70s. Now they had the whopper of all in a giant bill and me broke and to my then accountant it seemed the only defense was bankruptcy which meant I couldn't pay any of my bills. For months we were suddenly living a cash-only lifestyle. Spare change took on new meaning, eating out or movies were a luxury again.

Though I had acquired something I really wanted and believed the family deserved, bankruptcy had a definite effect on my frame of mind. It wasn't that the family was suffering a special strain- we were too well socially integrated to wind up on the street and we were pretty sure we'd get through it. But I had rarely before felt inadequate as a provider. I suddenly had a great sympathy for my father who worked constantly but was unable to move the family up the economic ladder.

The complexity of modern existence makes the life of a simple farmer seem enviable. You are independent, you have a range of survival skills and your fate is substantially in your hands. Your family members all have roles in ensuring the quality of your life together. Your adversaries are the weather and your own sloth or infirmity. In the city you depend on others for everything and work a monolithic job to pay for these goods and services. Then a robot replaces you and it's time to get the family back to the farm.

Compound

Danny O'Connor moved his family from Chicago to a property in Muir Beach, a place with an acre of lawn which they shared with the moles. He started holding regular volleyball games with the local volunteer firemen and "The Compound" became the place to be on the weekends. Rachel would make rafts of food, there would be sports on the radio and the gaming would go on from the AM until dark, sometimes 10 hours straight. The level of athleticism ranged from the completely inept to semi-pro Brazilian beach players who used questionable service techniques. We were supposed to 'self-enforce' the rules, which meant there were constant yelling matches and the occasional snit. Many of the participants were big and clumsy and injuries were common. There was no chivalry- if a woman stepped on the court she got the same brutal treatment. We became so addicted to the adrenaline that a Thursday night league started up, mostly comprised of the most macho players of which I considered myself one. It was during one of these matches when I noticed that the ball felt like it had a dent in it. Examination of the ball revealed no defect, then I saw that the last joint on my left little finger was flopped over and I couldn't straighten it. The next day I went to a doctor who told me I had a detached extensor tendon and I'd have to immobilize one of my important guitar fingers for at least 2 months. My volleyball career ended that day.

Athletics did not seem to run in my family. I don't remember ever seeing my parents run. Neither I nor my siblings excelled at any sport. Aside from occasional threats like going to the draft board I didn't have a whole lot of experience with extended rushes of adrenaline. Once I was forced into retirement from volleyball I was able to see that it brought out something dark and hostile in me and knew I and everyone else was better off without me in the game.

Apparently, there is such thing as adrenaline addiction. It is connected to a personality trait commonly known as 'thrill seeking' which is potentially inherited. But whether or not one has the disposition, the body makes its own drugs and loves it when you use them. What are those glands for if not to reenforce your behavior by making you feel strong or happy? Go glands, go!

Burning

I got it into my head to go to Burning Man and rented an SUV out of Reno then filled it with supplies and barterable items at a Walmart that seemed to exist solely for such purpose. The drive to Black Rock was by turns bleak and mystical- nothing, nothing... Pyramid Lake!... nothing, nothing. Past a truck stop and it finally looks like I'm getting close, which means the trip is about half over. After motoring onto the playa after what would be a typical friday on the 405, I roll around until I find a spot up near the 10 o'clock area of the onion that is the fragrant multilayered organism spawned by The Man. I'm next to a tent set up with what are already antique Atari consoles and not too far from that most execrable of phenomena, a rave camp which thunders mindless techno pretty much always. I head out to the playa and am struck first by the expanse of clear sky. It's my good fortune that conditions are perfect, the clay rock hard, the winds gentle. They are just starting the Wacky Races, not a single street legal vehicle amongst the 50 or so contestants. Not far away is a geodesic Thunderdome encrusted with rooters for the bungeed combatants. I go into a cowboy bar set up by some Texas burners and barter for a cocktail. Three giant military cargo planes from a nearby base buzz low over the playa and everybody cheers. On Saturday night, with much pomp and circumstance including semi-nude dancers and hundred foot pillars of flame, they burn The Man and since it is fireworks as well as a lot of fire I am in heaven in the desert.

It's especially hard to recall things with a lot of detail about a Burning Man experience. Aside from the general sensory assault and free liquor and stuff which you could barter for, you are encouraged in every possible way to get over yourself, which I am totally into. You kind of find out how liberal you actually are, whether you can accept and be accepted. There were probably things I could have easily done, but those were all opportunities to get real with myself and since it was my first BM I didn't get too crazy.

Black Rock is for a month a major city. It is created by the consent of those creating it. There is an inner circle of organizers and a mythical spokesperson (The Jack Rabbit) but there is no leader, no head of government. It makes you wonder if this could be a model for something more permanent. But everyone knows they are going back to the land of paved roads and showers and soft beds. Work and taxes. Responsibilities. Except for those lucky bastards who just go back to organizing next year's Burn.

Silly

In the 90s Silicone Alley was the NYC equivalent of the despicable remains of the era of innovation that began in a garage in San Mateo. Till Kruger got himself a second floor office space overlooking Broadway & Houston from where he conducted a design business funded by I have no idea what. One night Till invited me along to troll with the latest denizen to have secured a round of funding on a night of celebration. We met him and his retinue at a sushi restaurant so hip that it had no signage- you just had to discover the address. Everything was stupidly, unjustifyingly expensive and our host kept ordering tons of it, especially premium sake. The party then moved to a new S&M 'club' down the block from the Chelsea Hotel, which I assume is going to turn out like when Fredo takes Michael to a Havana freak show. Before long Mr. Lucky is suddenly shirtless in some sort of rack device being whipped by a latex-clad employee who I assume got a huge tip. I'm pretty sure none of his investors were part of the entourage, although I was a bit too grossed to find out what happened after I thence bid my adieu.

I've never been good at coming up with schemes to get rich. I've never even known how much money I have or how much debt I'm carrying since from the time I ever had any there's been an accountant to tend to it. "Rounds of investment" and "IPOs" were foreign concepts to me, that suddenly seemed like all anyone was talking about. I couldn't even figure out what these people were making that was worth so much before it was made.

It is easy to become rich (lottery ticket aside). You just have give up anything else of value and you can have that money. You remain focussed constantly on the goal of wealth to the detriment of everything and everyone else. You don't buy the things you really want, but instead adorn yourself with the accoutrements that impress others whose similar desire is to be pointlessly monied. You acquaint yourself not with people you like and respect, but with those who can aid you in your goal, which is not to accomplish anything in particular beyond being rich. You may actually find, if you bother to examine, that you are a miserable person but to have misgivings is to undercut the religious devotion you have to money. Mo' money, mo' problems but you ain't givin' up that gelt.

Marin

One day I went to pick Randy up from a 'play date' in Mill Valley. I had the driving instructions written out, but it would not have been too much of a challenge to find the huge house on a prominent and formerly quiet corner in the town. As I pulled into the drive there was an obvious frenzy of grounds renovation in front of a domicile on the scale of Willie Wonka's Chocolate Factory. I rounded the spacious drive and parked in front of the estimable staircase that led to the grand portico and rang the bell. A pleasant woman, The Woman of the House as opposed to a servant I presumed, let me in and called for the kids to present themselves. In the pregnant interval that accompanies child herding, the man of the house descended the stairway from heaven that flowed from the second floor and immediately impressed me with how short he was- I recall him as a slightly hirsute Dudley Moore (perhaps I'm being redundant). We shared some idle conversation which was inevitably to lead to implications on his part about what a smartypants investor he was and how simple it should be to own an outlandishly boorish house in what used to be an artists' retreat. Randy finally appeared and we beat a hasty exit that was supposed to disguise the creepy feeling that, well..., creeped over me.

When I first laid eyes on the homeowner, whose face or name I don't remember anymore, something seemed not to be exactly in perspective. This wasn't a normal house. This was a house built to a scale beyond the norm- this was a house for Andre The Giant, or a newly rich basketball player, way bigger than I was comfortable with. And yet this guy was not much more than 2/3 my size, not quite a dwarf but pushing it. I suppose he thought the ostentation would increase his stature, but in reality it made him look like more of a midget than ever.

When I realized that Marin was becoming a haven for those looking to overcome any manner of shortcoming by buying larger, driving faster, living ruder... well let's say the faint scribblings on the wall became that much more clearly etched. I didn't leave the mainland specifically because of the onslaught of feckless new-money idiots, but I can say with certainty they offered no reason to stay.

Toothless

We had about forty or so people come over to the island for the holiday and the property blessing. My mom and dad and brother and his family all made it which resulted in the closest thing to family reunion I could possibly stand. We tried to get someone to do a traditional ceremony (whatever that was- we'd never seen one before) but all the natives insisted on injecting some Calvinist missionary slant to it so we had to resort to a couple of more recent immigrants with a greater respect for the old ways (whatever they were). All the log boys spent the day laboring on the shed like a bunch of shirtless Amish barnraisers, and we finished just minutes before the ceremony was scheduled to begin. Most of us got dosed on mushrooms which kicked in perfectly around the time dinner had been served and the hula lady started her act by the light of a blissful sunset. The festivities went well into the night, including side trips to the beach to play imaginary volleyball and over to Bette's to jump in the pond and explore the mystery house by night. The entire week was packed with activities including a death march to Hanakapiai that finds the demons on Al's back instead of mine on the return trip. This has given me a cocky, no prisoners attitude as we head up to the falls a few days later through a creek bed near Kapa'a. It is a trek out of a Paradise Lost movie- precarious hillside stands of bamboo and muck, wild awapuhi for the sun and guavas for hunger, more muck, crystalline springs providing cool showers and feeding plants with leaves the size of rowboats, Till slipping and landing in muck up to his grinning neck, Bob tripping and giggling like he has been all week while he drops somebody's camera in the water. As we approach the streamhead the rocks are bigger and I am leaping longer distances, getting away with a lot of chances on the slippery boulders. John is about 50 feet behind me when I make the imprudent decision to bridge a couple of giant eggs and my face winds up were my feet should be. I realize instantly that for the first time, at the age of 47, I have busted a tooth out of my head. And as I stand there bleeding I realize that I am a mile and a half up the creek.

John is a nurse in the ER at a San Francisco hospital. I believe that witnessing my face-planting stunt may have upset him as much as me. For the intervening moments, then hours, then days and weeks I could easily replay the incident from my perspective and sympathize with him. But like childbirth the trauma loses vitality for me while he is permanently imprinted by the spectacle of my foolishness.

Though my injury was ultimately minor and may in the long run give me something goofy to do with my inevitably deteriorating dental condition, I probably came as close to killing myself in that moment as I ever would outside of an automobile. Life is always just a matter of inches once your head starts traveling at such speeds.

Baseball

Rex and Randy would toss a ball around on Sunshine Ave which basically meant that one of them would be down the hill and one up the hill so there was a great incentive not to let the ball go by if you were at the bottom. It also meant you had to have a good arm to get the ball back up the hill. Rex was just starting high school at Mount Tamalpais and the sports program had to charge for tickets to hire a 'citizen' baseball coach because there was no budget otherwise. Dave, then a meat purveyor, had actually been a professional baller so he knew what he was doing and could recognize talent. One day I went to pick Rex up after practice and Dave takes me aside and tells me that for his age, Rex has the softest hands he's ever seen, which freaks me out at first. Then I realize he is talking about how well he handles the ball (*see Sunshine Avenue). His opinion is that if Rex wanted to work hard enough he could possibly become a professional baseball player. At that moment the skies opened up and a heavenly host of angels announced that Rex might not wind up in jail like the rest of his feckless friends. It's a big decision for someone barely fifteen to make but there was nothing else in life he cared to do except tempt trouble so the family went all in. At least now we some guiding principle about where he should go to school and what was expected of him. The decision actually changed him.

When we found out about Rex's gift for baseball I had no idea how the game worked. Indeed, I found it almost as boring to watch as golf. Suddenly we had skin in the game. I had to learn to actually appreciate the game itself, not just root for one player. I, probably like most people, thought it was all about the hitter going long, the home run record, and felt that defensive skill was secondary. Rex could hit but his strength was on the field, so I began to realize that was the point- ball control. The batter is simply trying to take control from the defense, to put the ball in play, which is when the fun starts.

There was a time when if you asked a kid what he wanted to be when he grew up, the vast majority would say professional ball player. It looks so glamorous from the stands, and for a few players it is. But the math is cruel: there are 30 major league teams in the US which means if you want to be a starter, there are 30 of those jobs in the world. And those jobs rarely turn over- think of all the kids who got drafted by the Yankees hoping they would play shortstop after Jeter secured the position. And the draft is a horrifying experience to go through, watching years of work potentially amount to nothing. If you do get into the system, you are at the mercy of forces beyond your control and there is no assurance of advancement or placement. You're meat. Good luck kids!

Harry

My dad was always a tobacco smoker. Never cigarettes but pipes and sometimes cigars. Also, as he got older he developed a condition where he couldn't turn his head, which resulted in many parking lot episodes involving bumping and scraping and everyone trying to ignore it. He was not an aggressive driver but he was overconfident in his abilities and on one visit to Lake Hill he almost got himself and my mom killed when his slowed reactions put him in the wrong lane on a blind curve. During our Kauaian Labor Day celebration wherein I smashed my face on a rock it had also been revealed that my dad had a lump in his throat and would be be going in for tests when he got home. Sure enough, it turned out to be malignant and he had surgery to remove the growth, which went well enough but for the fact that surgeon didn't realize that he wouldn't be able to push Harry's head back to look inside (*see calcified vertibrae) and just started scooping stuff out until it looked not like cancer. A bunch of nerve tissue must have been in there because he lost control of his vocal chords and had to rasp in a way that sounded like Donald Duck. It also affected his epiglotis and about six months after the operation he aspirated food, contracted pneumonia and went into the hospital. Within two weeks he was gone.

Harry and I had made peace with each other long before he died, so there was no great drama at the bedside the last time I saw him. I thanked him for fathering me and enduring me and reassured him that I did love him because he deserved it. Somehow my burial of the past allowed us to reboot and appreciate each other in a way that gave us a closure that no one else in the family seemed to be able to find.

Family is the fancy name we use for brood colony, that complex connection of relatives that would otherwise be an ant farm. Some have deep roots and its members can trace their lineage back centuries, as if that mattered. Your life is going to be about your immediate family, parents, siblings, uncles and aunts and cousins by the dozens and the precious, precious grandparents from which endless bounties flow.

Move

The Bay Area was starting to get a little weird, especially at the nexus of Sausalito. There was the southern meme, the tech boom that used to be about ideas but was now becoming investment bankers flying through the Waldo Tunnel in a new Lexus with a cell phone glued to their ear. Then there was Tha Gangsta scene in Oakland across the bay where festering unrest and a resentment of those same speculators looked to boil over any minute. And right next door was Marin City, home to Tupac- never was there such a stark contrast between abutting communities. The well off white kids of our neighborhood started to think gang behavior was hip and petty criminality was a rite of passage. Rex was still being tempted by his contemporaries who were getting in ever more serious trouble. We were experiencing lean times and the Banana Belt was becoming a luxury so we decided that at the end of the school year we would move the family to Kauai. Since we had so many local connections and because I needed a pied a terre when touring we found an affordable loft off the Mission in a filthy dogleg alley haunted by a constant stream of junkies but was otherwise a pretty good location. Our realtor on the island found us a couple of cheap rentals, a small one-story for Bean and a two-story across the street for the rest of us. We packed a container with possessions, cashed in the savings bonds Baba had bought for me when I was little, and bid the mainland Aloha.

I don't really like moving, even if I am looking forward to where I'm moving to. Reassessing everything you own to see if it still has a place in your life or whether it goes in the dumpster. All the crating and wrapping material that eventually winds up in a landfill at the final destination. The months it takes to settle back into some normalcy and feel like you are not just in a house but a home. If it's a long move you have to find new friends and new haunts, ingratiate yourself to the locals and adjust to what may be a whole other philosophy about driving on the highway.

The lifestyle of a traveling musician is perfectly suited to the nomadic personality. Some people are naturally rootless and restless and playing for even a very small audience is better than being a hobo. You might have a home but you don't invest much in it and don't miss it when you're not there. As such you might as well play any old crap just so long as it keeps you moving on down the highway and Lord, aren't there enough of those songs. May as well just get a job with the carnival.

Kauai

The first time I went to Kauai was on the recommendation of Susan Lee. My goal was to combine a little spiritual questing with an escape from Bebe which would involve as much distance as possible. Now decades later I am transplanting my entire existence to this faraway place. Randy is still pretty young and adaptable but Rex isn't taking the move well which is compounded by an unprovoked altercation with a local boy who thought Rex was giving him 'stink eye'. Also, he is attending school on Oahu which means he is cut off from the family except for weekends. The Hale-Bopp comet is a constant fixture in the sky, something most people on the planet can't see because of light pollution. The island is still recovering from Hurricane Iniki and a significant segment of the North Shore population is either contractors from the mainland or the crews of Jurassic Park or 8 Days 7 Nights. Amelia's, the little bar at the Princeville airport became the hottest road house in all of the islands. After about a year in the house on Victoria Loop we found another larger and nicer place nearby for a reasonable rent and from that point on we were living on a golf course with an unobstructed view of the mountains. Flights were still coming in to Princeville from Honolulu so Rex comes home on Friday night and goes back on Sunday unless there are baseball games. It's a different routine living in such a rural place but life is not boring and nature is spectacular in all its beauty and danger,

I would regularly go out to the property on Wailapa and spend hours with a walking mower on about 2 acres of it, cutting thousand-foot swaths in one direction then back the other, all the while imagining every detail of the home I would build there one day. We were looking to get rid of the Lake Hill property, the only real estate I actually owned so I was standing on what was a homesteaders lot in the westernmost part of the country. I am ready to accept this. I am a haole homesteader.

I do not believe in a deity with a human personality, but there is an argument for a grand creator. All things in the human realm exist as a result of a series of processes. First, the possibility of a thing existing has to be believed in, that there is the power for such a thing to be. Then that thing must be visualized in ever more minute detail so that the thought of it is comparable to the real thing. That is when mystical laws take over and matter starts to take on the form of this thing. Why wouldn't this be true, why can't most people get what they want this way? Plainly because as much as they want the thing they don't believe they can get it, haven't really figured out what it is, and give up before it can become a reality.

Drowned

We were in Hanapepe to watch Rex play a special weekend of inter-island baseball, enjoying a break from the endless soggy weather of that winter. We're packing up when Al gets a phone call of obviously serious portent. He hangs up and says "The news is not good. Eric Myers drowned". Apparently he was hoping to catch some lobsters in the reef near his newly-purchased property. In his inexperience he had been sucked out through a channel in the lava reef, knocked unconscious and never came up. His body was found some hours later. The drive back to the North Shore was all shock and numbness and waiting for the pain to really hit. We got filled in on the details. The next day I went to the property and started mowing. My neighbor Ken came over on his riding mower, offered condolences and cut a couple rows out of solidarity. Though I spent most of the day there, I went home not feeling a whole lot better. Eric's parents came over to collect his body and we had a little memorial on the property he had bought with the money his dad had lent him. It was pretty dignified until I started blubbering about how paternal I felt about him which must have been awful for his family to hear but I couldn't help it.

When I got the news of my bestie Randy's suicide I hadn't seen him or heard from him in a long time. I couldn't imagine my lifelong friend taking his life without reaching out to me. I was as angry as I was heartbroken and probably thought I could have had an effect on the outcome. An unexpected death like Eric's was just plain confounding and unfair. There was never anything to be done except mourn. Once I started I found it hard to stop.

It is a heartening thing to see yourself in someone as they start to flower. You often meet peers and discover a lot in common, but you have already found your paths. To see yourself in someone much younger who has no cynicism makes you feel like there is a clean slate, that ideally they won't make the mistakes you did. The world is wide and untainted and you are invincible... perhaps.

Saugerties

'Woodstock 94' turned out great for me. I had my own tent/pavilion in the middle of the techno village, plenty of time for the crew to set up and tweak the pod, a permanent trailer of our own and the run of the highways so we could sleep at home. We were up and running a few days before the gates so I got to explore most of the huge site before the rain and chaos. Not having made the first festival and therefor having no point of reference it all looks pretty bitchin' to me. We're about a third of a mile from the big stage which is about a quarter mile from the slightly less big stage and the place is so gigantic that I think it's going to look empty with anything under a million people. By Friday it isn't even half that but the place is packed and it's a muddy madhouse. By Saturday evening I've completed about 9 shows and I decide to go check out Nine Inch Nails on the main stage. As it turns out, it's no Woodstock back there. They switch passes and access privileges every twenty minutes and every act that goes on wants security to behave like they're headlining Shea Stadium. I watch the Nails do their makeup by wallowing in a bog and flinging muck on innocent bystanders. I'm about to get booted out of the stage area when Michael Lang rescues me and I get to see a couple of numbers from the wings. I'm late for my own show so I slime skate over to the 'Rainbow Bridge' which is so clogged with people wandering in aimless currents that I wind up slogging through the swollen creek and maneuvering the maze of soaked tents and sleeping bags before showing up about 40 minutes late for what would be the last show. By Sunday the pavilion is totally given over to squatters escaping the rain. We don't even bother to show up.

Everything I know about the original Woodstock I got from the movie since I was busy in the studio with my very first production. Others were able to compare the 'vibes' but I was never tempted to do so. It was my chance to wallow in a memory that I never had which I guess made it easier for me to enjoy the whole thing. Whatever music I got to hear was whatever fragments got carried by the wind over the trees so I was spared the agony of sitting through some contemporary act as deadly as, say, Ten Years After. That probably would have been The Cranberries.

There's no doubt in my mind that the first Woodstock festival was different. Again I find myself so far ahead of the curve that while everyone was complaining about the high corporate profile and the seeming fecklessness of the 90s crowd, I was beyond my natural cynicism to the point that I could occasionally enjoy myself without thinking about it. I would do it again, even considering the likelihood that should the pattern hold I would be miserable while everyone else is having a blast.

Keoni

Since Randy was still elementary age he went to Hanalei School because it was geographically closest to Princeville. He hooked up with a chubby little kid named Keoni who started lingering regularly for dinner at our house. His father was a character actor who had run out of gigs and was divorced from his mom who lived in Arizona. Apparently his usual dinner ritual was accompanying dad to the bar at Chuck's Grill and all the cocktail snacks you could eat, after which dad passes out and leaves you to fend for yourself until next Happy Hour. One day at about the age of ten Keoni woke up to find his dad had succumbed to an untreated sepsis and then went to the bus stop for school. At some point someone thought to inquire about his mood. He couldn't go back to the house where his dead father lay so he came to live with us. That's when we learned about his 'upbringing' and all the tricks he developed in order to survive what was either abuse or neglect from those who were supposed to protect and nurture him. He had been previously arrested (at nine?!?) for selling hotel shampoo bottles filled with liquor he stole from his dad at the school bus stop, this to get money for lunch which no one ever made for him. Whatever the 'street' was on the North Shore, Keoni was from it. It was a constant struggle to get him to trust us, expecting at some point we would also abandon him. Randy's friendship with him wasn't surviving the idea of his being a brother with such a different view of family. We were all tested.

Taking Keoni in was not an easy decision. A lot of people advised us against it, citing statistics that pointed to an inevitable intervention by the system. But the idea of reenforcing to a neglected kid that nobody really wants you was something I couldn't get comfortable with. I guess in some way I took his plight personally. I thought our family had the strength to help him overcome the worst that life could inflict. It was hubris. We could not undo what others had already done.

In Hawaiian culture there is the concept of 'ohana', which could literally be translated as 'family' but is more complicated than that. It is an aspiration for an all inclusive unity that puts a special emphasis on respect for the elderly and love and protection for the keiki, the little ones. If you can express these things then you are ohana. If you are selfish and cold and disrespectful you will never be ohana and never be happy in the Islands.

Reunion

Liv contacted me out of the blue while we were both in LA. She was no longer a little girl, but nearly as tall as I and as beautiful in real life as all the pictures we had seen of her. We had a private reunion, then she wanted me to meet her boyfriend Joaquin Phoenix. He was very shy and polite and he and Liv seemed to be happy so I was happy for them. I was staying in Eric Gardner's pool house in Los Feliz and asked them up to hang out for a while. We smoked some pot which loosened Liv and me up and eased our conversation. I notice Joaquin is out by the pool focussed on something in the water and he's obviously agitated about it. We join him to find that a moth has flown into the pool and he is fretting over whether to rescue it and how he might accomplish that- this is one sensitive guy. Liv would eventually reconnect with everyone in the family, which was especially gratifying to her brothers who barely remembered her and didn't know what to say when others asked about her. We had our little girl back.

After so many years I was not sure what to expect from Liv. She was a different person and it could have been a long, uncomfortable process to heal a protracted separation. But she needed to get over it as much as I and when we hugged for the first time it's like a fire is burning away the past. We hold each other for what seems like hours, heart to heart like when we fell asleep together on Annie's couch. We are normalized, back to square one.

It is remarkable how a wound that seems will never heal can be cured with a bit of penicillin. Closure is penicillin for the soul, literally closing the wound. Perhaps a scar remains but that will fade.

Emergency

I had to go to Bearsville to produce a record for a interesting new act, ironically in what used to be the Utopia Video studio. Things started out promising but technical and interpersonal issues began to take over. It became apparent that the frontman and principle songwriter had worked in the mailroom of a record company which inspired him to challenge every suggestion I would make (simple things like don't change person in the middle of a phrase) which led me to unfortunately conclude that he always wanted to be the producer. When I could not convince him to perform a vocal instead of pasticching a vocal my usefulness became moot and I turned the rest of the recording process over to the engineer.

Meanwhile, it is the end of a season of SNL and I arrange for Hal Wilner to get me and some guests in- Jane and Virginia looking very well turned out. We strut into the after party and Hal introduces me to some of the cast members, including Tina Fey who went to my high school. I'm approached by one of the writers from the show who tells me they have a new series called That 70s Show and the first episode is about kids going to a Todd Rundgren concert. I return to the attic room of Albert's guest house feeling pretty fly. Next morning is Mothers Day and I call Michele to tell her how smashing things went the night before when she declares she is 'leaving' me, whatever that means, for another man I have never met. I ask if she has introduced the kids to him and she had. I beseech if she is serious and she proclaims she is, and I can't figure out what I've done and go silently crazy for a little while after we hang up. Then I get on a plane.

My first reaction was that our children would be thrown into that world of self-blame and choosing sides and all the horrible things that go along with adults suddenly behaving like adolescents. Setting the stage for future relationships that had failure prebuilt because of the fact that the most 'sensible' people in the room suddenly don't understand each other.

For some, the loss of a loved one's faith in you may simply diminish that person in your eyes and you may console yourself with the conviction that they just didn't understand you. Spitefully, you might banish them or bury them, had you the power. Maybe the last thing you do is examine your foundation, assure yourself that it is built on... Unobtainium.

Hadj

The trip back to Kauai was interminable. The connecting flight to Honolulu I had hoped to catch got cancelled and I had to stew around the terminal all night snatching small moments of sleep. By the time Michele picked me up in Lihue it was early afternoon. We made some small talk on the way to Wailapa but I don't think either of us knew what the agenda might be. We go up to the bedroom and I ask her to sit on the couch. I get on my knees and confess my selfishness. Without any expectation of her reaction, I ask her to marry me. She will. I spend another few days at home before returning to Bearsville to finish Splender, the whole time wondering if she might change her mind so I decide to fix a date- my 50th birthday. Barely a month away.

I had been proud that I had kept a family together without the benefit of marriage. I believed it proved my commitment, especially as so many of our friends had failed to make marriage work. But I was also overly proud of my independence, doing things my way even if it isolated me from the family. Michele wound up doing much of the grunt work and I convinced myself she enjoyed it. I had encouraged her to give up her career while I kept mine, rationalizing that I made the money that underwrote our lifestyle. When that became difficult I would become sullen and introverted and refused to share myself.

Marriage can make you different or at least feel different. It can be simple as getting used to referring to your girlfriend as your wife. Some will have a greater sense of security while others will suddenly feel trapped. It may signal the loss of youth or the end of a long quest for happiness. Maybe it's for the dowery or the keys to the kingdom. If nothing at all changed, what would be the the point?

Wedding

The morning of my 50th birthday I got up at dawn and went out to Aaron's place in Wainihai to collect taro leaves for the laulau, stooping through the muck of the taro patch in a haze. By the time we got back it was clean up, get into the car and hightail it to the courthouse as Michele and I wanted to officialize the deed before having to deal with the collective expectations. By the time we got back most of the neighborhood had turned out and David K. and the boys were putting the finishing touches on a crude version of the stage we had always intended to build. Thereon we assembled ourselves, Rex, Randy, Rebop, Keoni and Bean and took turns addressing the folks (or not), declared ourselves wed and got on with the party. So, as previously agreed, I got drunk as a sailor, retired to the yurt where resided the tat artist hired to ink anyone who dared and got my ring finger tattooed with Michele's name in a design I devised on the spot and which came out a little blurry because I was so drunk and high I kept getting distracted and flailing around. Late that night we attempted to sleep in our bridal tent while Bill Kreutzman jammed about 20 feet away until nearly dawn.

When it was time to acknowledge this obvious milestone in front of about 200 onlookers from the little stage in the hollow overlooking Crater Hill and the Kilauea River I pretty much created the epitaph of my single life on the fly. I confessed that I had withheld myself from my family for reasons that I might have justified, but that would not withstand the fact that I had coerced them into my world view and left them to simply deal with it. Yes I loved them and they knew that but they did not have all of me and they knew that as well. Whilst I proclaimed to love them above all, I glorified my work as justification for remaining aloof.

Do people really change? Can you transform, forget every fantasy or grudge or heartbreak, start over and become a new person? One that even you yourself believe in? That is why the story ends here. The Individualist, having served his purpose, is history. Henceforth, the tale is of another Todd. Who may seemingly have a much more boring existence unless something very unexpected happens. Which likely will.

Epilog

I wasn't yet fifty when I first undertook to write my story. I cannot say that I slaved over it since quite obviously it would have been completed long ago. In the end it has been an act of constant surrender. I was constantly importuned about the existence of it, the progress of it, the nature of it, whether there should be photos, yadayada. Ultimately I decided that above all it should be pithy, the kind of reading that my attention-challenged mentality could enjoy on, say, a flight from New York to Sydney.

Even in this I strive not to tell the story as one would expect. I was always trying to balance between what I wanted to say and what I would be expected to reveal. How much detail do I want to struggle to remember for the prurient curiosity of an audience that I have gone to great lengths to assure that I Do Not Take Requests.

Your first purpose in life is to become yourself, to decide what you want to be and commit all your efforts into becoming that. But at some point you will have to move on to another phase in which you take what you have made of yourself and commit it to the service of others. That is when you realize how many connections you've made, the vast network you've become a part of. You are no less yourself. You are much more than yourself.

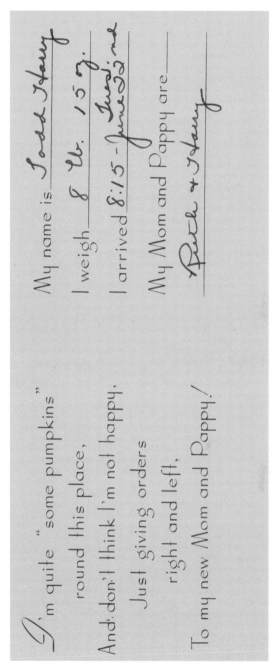

I'm quite "some pumpkins"
round this place,
And: don't think I'm not happy,
Just giving orders
right and left,
To my new Mom and Pappy!

My name is _Todd Harry_

I weigh _8 lb. 15 oz._

I arrived _8:15 - June 30 me_

My Mom and Pappy are _____
Ruth & Harry

Family Photo

UNTO US
A pumpkin is born?

Family Photo

TRUST
I wonder what happened immediately after this picture.

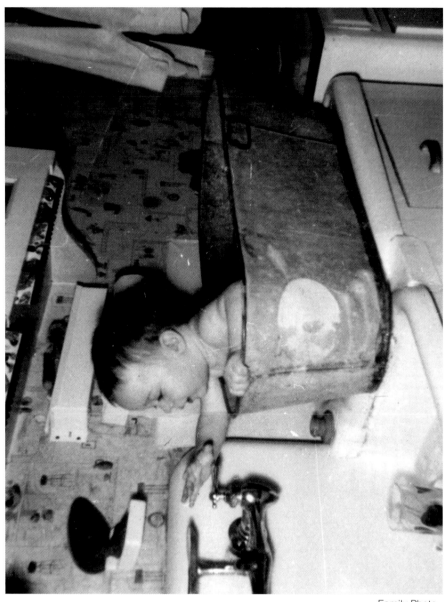

Family Photo

BATH TIME
In the zinc.

Family Photo

WESTBROOK PARK
circa 1949

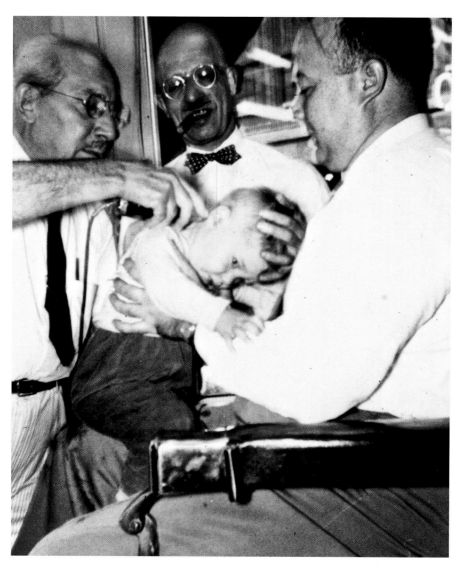

THE HORROR
Just before the police arrive in response to the screaming.

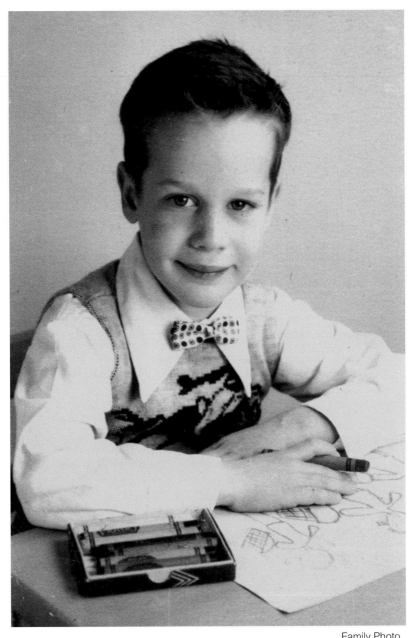

Family Photo

FIRST GRADE
Honor student or bad seed?

NUCLEAR FAMILY
Myself, Lynette, June, Robin and a ghost in the background.

TROOP 111
Randy Read top left, myself top right.

WOODY'S TRUCK STOP
Alan Miller, Kenny Radeloff & myself. Which one is Woody?

NAZZ
Carson, Stewkey, myself & Thom. Matching suits, off the rack.

CARNABY STREET
American fops abroad- no more matching suits.

13TH STREET
My first place and the doorway where DeNiro shot Keitel in Taxi Driver.

STAGE FRIGHT
In the prop tent with John Taplin, Robbie Robertson and John Simon.

PATTI SMITH
We were kids.

Philip D'Angelo

SALES
Hunt and Tony and me in Cleveland.

THE BALLAD
Mocking up my second album cover.

INCOGNITO
With Bebe Buell.

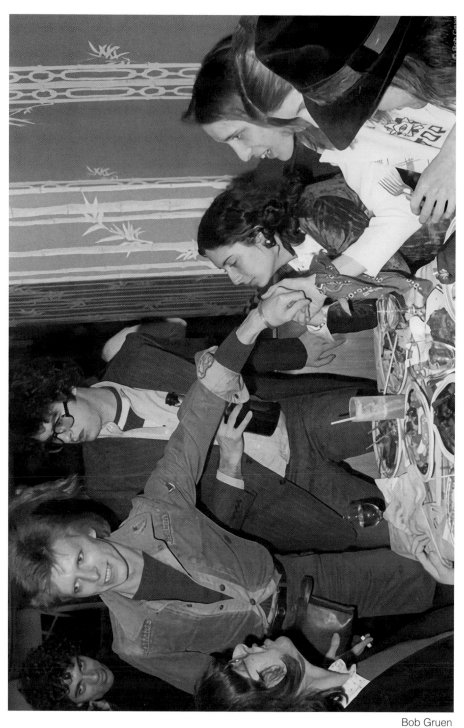

BOWIE
Kissing the Duke's ring in Max's KC back room.

ALICE
Soon to be related by canine birth.

FREDDIE
After Queen's NYC premier.

IGGY

After his show upstairs at Max's. Note the various scars and bandages.

SECRET SOUND
John Siegler, Ralph Schuckett, me, Moogy Klingman & Kevin Ellman.

TR's UTOPIA
We decide to tie the knot and declare ourselves a band (Roger Powell included).

VENUS
I am becoming much less self-conscious of the camera.

NICKY NICHOLS
The pride of Enid, Oklahoma… whether they know it or not.

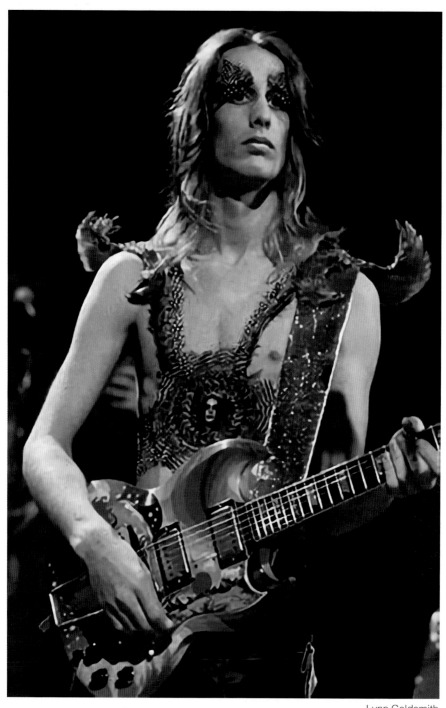

FRIGHTENING THE CHILDREN
And getting a toehold on the Japanese market.

NEW YORK DOLLS
Just some guys from the neighborhood.

OLD MACDONALD
And I swore I would never wear denim.

UTOPIA V2
We are deadly serious.

REINCARNATED
Maybe not so serious.

Eric Gardner

MEATLOAF
An unauthorized version of Paradise By The Dashboard Light.

Eric Gardner

IAN HUNTER
On tour supporting independent presidential candidate John Anderson.

Alan Mills

A STAR IS BORN
Liv in her only fully nude appearance.

BEAN
Who rode into my life on a unicorn.

WHITE FOLKS
Paul Fishkin surrounded by Flo and Eddie and The Hello People.

KELLY
Backstage with Bean.

Family Photo

REX
Like father, like son.

NUCLEAR FAMILY
Me, Rex and Bean, carefree.

Family Photo

BFFS
Randy Read and I in a final photo op.

RANDY
My best friend's namesake, and tough as nails.

THE GODFATHER
Joel Tornabene frightening the children.

RUNDGRENS
A rare reunion… can you feel the joy?

MICHELE
Third time's a charm.

PIMPIN'
This is what a millenial family looks like.

THE MOTHERSHIP
Crash lands somewhere in Tokyo.

FRIENDS IN HIGH PLACES
Tim Leary, me and Don Was at the Individualist rollout party.

THE GARDNERS ENTERTAIN
Me, Eric and Janis Gardner, Little Richard and Phil Spector.

AND THEN THERE WERE THREE
Rebop finally weighs enough to come home.

Family Photo

FATHERHOOD
Back to work everybody.

CLAN RUNDGREN
Rebop, Michele, me, Randy, Rex and Keoni on our wedding day.